Echoes of Old Norfolk

The Author   (Photo: *Terry Burchell*)

Echoes of
Old Norfolk

Robert Bagshaw

Cover Illustration: River Bure at Buxton.
Photo: The Author.

By the Same Author:

Poppies To Paston.
Toothy Goes To War.
Norfolk Remembered.
More Memories of Norfolk.

ISBN   Hardback: 0 900616 49 0
        Softback: 0 900616 48 2

        Printed and published by
        Geo. R. Reeve Ltd., 9-11 Town Green, Wymondham, Norfolk.

CONTENTS

ILLUSTRATIONS

ILLUSTRATIONS (continued)

FOREWORD

By John Kett

"ECHOES OF OLD NORFOLK" ... what an evocative title! It certainly sets memories stirring for me, childhood memories of the first echoes that awakened me in the early morning when old Matthew trudged past on his way to the farm. Soon after would come the plod of horses and the rumble of a tumbril on the rough road, perhaps the confused sound of cows being driven to pasture, with the cowman calling, a dog barking, country sounds to be repeated throughout the day until at last dusk fell, and a thrush echoed his own sweet notes from the top of the old pear tree.

But these echoes of mine belong to the early 'twenties, to a home by an old fen road in West Norfolk. Bob Bagshaw's echoes cover practically a life-time and come from town and village, farm and field, from men and women he has known over the years. Some are well-known, others hardly heard of outside their own locality, but all, as he puts it, are "too good to be forgotten". They speak all manner of dialects, these acquaintances of his, and their voices are often an important part of the characters in this procession that he has marshalled so capably for our benefit, and recorded with such skill and care. Our northern neighbours say, "There's nowt so queer as folk"; as depicted by Bob "there's nowt so interesting".

Many place-names come out to meet us from these pages, Norwich and Sandringham, Tottington and Howe, and we know that in every place there are more people to meet, more achievements to hear of, locally or far afield. Sometimes these appear unimportant, but in every case there is human interest, and tales of unusual accomplishments, of service to others, and praiseworthy actions which all too often are forgotten. "Some there be which have no memorial"; Bob provides one in this book.

Readers "of riper years" are in for a treat as they scan these pages, where words and photographs take us back to the past, perhaps to a village entertainment where Sidney Grapes entertained us about half a century ago, to days when people sang "Wonderful Amy" after that solo flight to Australia, or to

"Children's Hour" sessions with Romany. We recall our long-suffering schoolteachers when we read of dedicated Hilda Rump, and remember with gratitude public-spirited people like Anna Smith – the salt of the earth! Old familiar faces from our own memories join Bob's cavalcade, and as the pages are turned our pleasure increases.

Back in the pre-TV days we learned a good deal of poetry; to be able to "do a recitation" was a useful accomplishment when we had to make our own entertainment. We would display our youthful ability by our own fireside, or at the long-awaited Chapel anniversary, or perhaps on the stage at a village concert. One by one we said our piece and possibly received more applause than we deserved. One poem I recall from those times was "Abou Ben Adhem" by Leigh Hunt. Abou was visited by none other than the Recording Angel, and made a request that he should be listed as one who loved his fellow men. This surely applies to Bob Bagshaw; the secret of his ability to produce such a book as this stems from his affection for mankind, his great capacity for friendship. Those who have read his earlier books, or have heard his talks on Radio Norfolk, will be aware of this quality and will welcome this heart-warming addition to the literature of Norfolk, by a Norfolk man.

1

The Way We Were

Whatever you are − Be that.
Whatever you say − Be true.
Straightforwardly act;
Be honest in fact;
Be nobody else but you.

Lines written by a mother in her
young son's autograph album,
September 22nd, 1926.

CHAPTER 1

A Manner of Speaking

It has long been said that Norfolk folk have a great liking for "doing different". I am not sure that I accept this accusation – indeed, I like to think that we are the normal ones and it is the rest of the country that is out of step. When it comes to a question of speech, however, it is a different matter, for we have always had a highly individual way with words. We slaughter our consonants and play havoc with our vowels, and the result is a unique manner of speech which defies imitation by anybody not fortunate enough to have been born and raised in this fair county of ours.

There is another way in which the Norfolk dialect is unique, and this is best illustrated, I believe, by telling the story of an incident that took place in Norwich some years ago. It was at the time when the self-erecting umbrella had just been introduced but, as most local people had not heard of its existence, they were still going through the age-old process of pushing up their brollies by hand. At the time in question, however, a smartly-dressed man who stood on Gentleman's Walk had one of the new inventions and, when a shower of rain started to fall, just a quick press of the button was all that was needed to erect the umbrella. Nearby was a little old country lady who stood transfixed by this amazing piece of magic. Then, almost in disbelief, she said:

"Dew that dew that?"

"That dew," replied the man.

Now, I know of no other place in the world where it is possible to carry on a complete conversation using just two words.

In its broadest form, our manner of speech is almost unintelligible to outsiders; they criticise it, not knowing that they would have to go a long way before they heard purer English than that spoken by some of the older folk in these parts. We stand accused of not opening our mouths sufficiently wide when speaking – our natural East Anglian reticence, perhaps; or could it be to guard against the prevailing east wind? Whatever the reason, the result is that we tend to swallow our consonants and endow our vowels with strange-sounding qualities unrecognisable by strangers.

It is not easy to reproduce these sounds on the printed page, for the Norfolk dialect is purely oral in origin – it has always been simply a spoken means of communication and, though many have tried to produce it in written form, there are simply not enough phonetic symbols to do it full justice.

If we start with the letter 'a' we are in immediate trouble. The Reverend Robert Forby, Rector of Fincham in the early 1800s, collected together some 2,000 words and phrases in his *Vocabulary of East Anglia,* and it was his considered opinion that the Norfolk 'a' sounds "like the bleating of a very young lamb" – long drawn out and rhyming with 'fair' or 'dare'. In writing, it is usually represented by 'aa', so that 'don't be late' becomes 'don't yew be laate'.

Then we have 'e', which can become either 'i' or 'u' – hence 'get in the shed' becomes 'git yew in the shud'.

Our 'i' is slightly less of a nuisance, but 'o' is the worst troublemaker of all. Hence, 'nothing' becomes 'naathin'; 'hope' becomes 'hoop'; and a 'road' becomes a 'rood' (rhyming with 'good'). And when they come in pairs they turn into a 'u', as with 'fule' for 'fool'.

In our treatment of consonants it is little less than open warfare. At best they are pronounced in the softest possible form; at worst they are totally eliminated. No true native of Norfolk can roll his 'r's', so he pretends that they just don't exist – I, myself, admit to having great difficulty with the word 'squirrel'. But the most blatant example of all is our dropping of 't's', as when a Norfolk child asks for 'a bi' o' bread an' bu''er'. Then there is the classic tale of the schoolmaster – himself a true son of Norfolk – endeavouring to improve the basic English pronunciation of his young charges.

"Don't say be''er," he implored. "Say bet-ter".

"Bet-ter," repeated his obedient pupils.

"Thass more like it," said the teacher. "Thass much be''er".

Of all the consonants, however, there is one to which the citizens of Norwich and Norfolk each give their own individual treatment – the letter 'h'. While the city folk go merrily along swallowing each one as it comes along, their country cousins make an exception by emphasising them and, indeed, sticking in an extra one when the opportunity presents itself. To the uninitiated, the added habit of running the words into each other confuses things even more. The Norwich man's question, 'evyer'ungyer'atup?' becomes more understandable with the county man's more deliberate 'hev-yer-hung-yer-hat-up?'.

The late Eric Fowler delighted in recalling the occasion when, as he made his way to the Press Office in London Street, he was approached by a stranger with the request for directions to Largo Lane. Eric was puzzled until he suddenly realised that the required thoroughfare was, in fact, Lower Goat Lane.

I suppose it is the intricacies of our dialect which prevent anybody other than natives of the county from speaking it properly. I can recall just one 'foreigner' who could give a pretty fair representation of the Norfolk sound, and he is an Australian – the entertainer Rolf Harris. Whenever television brings us an offering which includes supposedly Norfolk people, we are almost invariably treated to the now familiar Mummerset sound, which makes each character sound like a blithering idiot. I recall one such television presentation which I endured for something like two hours until the one and only highlight appeared on the screen, and there, amongst the credit titles, was: 'Dialect Adviser – So-and-so'. The man's name was not familiar to me, and I was left wondering where he had been when the film was made!

Even worse than the desecration of our dialect by outsiders is the mutilation inflicted upon it by people who really ought to know better. For many years one of this county's better-known men of business has been dispatching his products to all points of the compass with the exhortation that they are 'bootiful'. Now, far be it from me to suggest that his turkeys are anything but beautiful, but every man with Norfolk blood in his veins knows that the first syllable of that adjective rhymes with 'new', whilst the 't' is softened to such an extent as to be almost inaudible. I am sure Mr. Matthews' turkeys are, indeed, bew'iful.

Then there are the television commercials which, for a number of years, have been proclaiming the virtues of Colman's Mustard – but pronouncing it as Coleman's. Surely they must know that Coleman's was the other Norwich company, which gave Wincarnis Tonic Wine to the world! Surely they should also know that the first syllable of the name rhymes with 'doll' and not 'dole'.

I suffered the irritation of these advertisements with ill-concealed disgust, but a friend of mine, a true man of Norfolk although now exiled in Gloucestershire, decided that action was

Col rhymes with doll;

Cole with dole.

called for. He wrote a letter of complaint to the company and, in due course, received a reply from no less a person than the Advertising Manager.

"You are quite right," said he. "But we are trying to perpetuate the accent of a Norwich TOFF in the twenties".

Those were his very words. And my friend's reaction?

"I give up," he said.

But pronunciation is merely one part of our manner of speech, for there is also the important matter of vocabulary. Visitors soon come to terms with such words as 'dwile' and 'mawther', but there has always been a vast array of others which have been in common usage over the centuries. Many of these sprang from the countryside and reflected Norfolk's close association with the land and the flora and fauna which were part of the country scene. It is here that much change has taken place, going hand-in-hand with the countryman's drift from the land. There has been great change in our manner of speaking during the past sixty years, and Broad Norfolk is not nearly as broad now as it was in my early years. It is now a great joy to meet one of the old-timers who still speaks in the only way he has ever known; it is sheer delight to suddenly hear the sound of long-forgotten words which were once an everyday feature of one's boyhood.

Above all, it is soothingly reassuring to hear the peculiar local turn of phrase which was unique to every true man of Norfolk. It is a strange up-and-down intonation of words and phrases, attractive yet by no means musical. It is this strange rhythm of our way of speaking which defies imitation. Impersonators may master the accent and the vocabulary, but the way in which the phrases are strung together is an inborn thing – it cannot be taught.

I suppose it is the difficulties of our dialect that have prevented its countrywide acceptance – after all, there is little point in proclaiming the attractions of one's homeland if your audience cannot understand the language in which you speak. Thomas Hardy did it for the West Country, and Robert Burns for Scotland. Perhaps it is simply the fact that our mode of speech lacks the musical quality of the Celts!

Nevertheless, there have been many sons (and daughters) of Norfolk who, either by word of mouth or by the written word, have proclaimed their pride in the county of their birth. One or two have briefly flirted with the adulation of national fame, but most have contented themselves with a more regional audience.

CHAPTER 2

Spreading The Word

James Spilling had a way with words, which was just as well, for he was the first Editor of the *Eastern Daily Press* more than a century ago. He must surely have been a good choice for the job, for he was a professional writer with the heart of a countryman and a never-wavering love for his home county. Furthermore, he had a special affection for the Norfolk dialect and took it as a personal affront when anybody saw fit to ridicule it.

In his fictional writings he invented the character of Giles, a typical Norfolk countryman, into whom he projected much of himself. He wrote a splendid scene in which Giles, offended by criticism of his accent by Londoners, is consoled by his friend Timothy Tickleboy:

Yow shud a heer'd my mawther
She say, yow heer them London chaps
Wot sing on Yarmouth beach,
Then yow will see and werry sune
Which is the rummest speech.
Yars, or them Cockney chaps wot cum
And kick up such a duller
In murderin' that poor letter H,
So doant yow mind a titty bit
As yow stand there a-garpin
But let 'em know ower Norfolk tongue
Will stan' theer jeers and larfin'.

Then, of course, there were those men who, in the twenties and early thirties, appeared at concerts all over the county in the guise of Norfolk dialect comedians. They were many and varied, but the two whom I recall with the greatest affection were, in fact, incredibly similar. They both appeared in similar garb – the miller's smock, the farmhand's neckerchief and the floppy hat – and they both had that rugged, weather-beaten face and the kind of smile that made their audiences eager to laugh even before they started their routine. What is more, they frequently told the same stories – but this merely added to the fun. Familiarity with the jokes meant that the audience, aware of what the ending would be, would burst into peals of laughter half way through. Then up would go the speaker's forefinger and, with a knowing smile, there came the admonition: "Now hold yew hard, my ole bewties!" It was all great fun, for the entertainer and his listeners were laughing in unison.

Looking back at the memory of those two men, it is difficult to say whether one was better than the other, for there was so little to choose between them. Yet today one has been largely forgotten while the other has become almost a part of Norfolk folklore.

The forgotten man was George Smith, who farmed not many miles outside North Walsham and was, indeed, the brother of our cubmistress, the much-loved Gladys Smith. The one whose memory lives on is Potter Heigham's favourite son, Sidney Grapes, and his lasting fame springs from the fact that, unlike George Smith, he burst into print. The spoken word is a transient thing; the written word has far greater permanence, and Sidney Grapes' writings are still eagerly snapped up from the shelves of second-hand bookshops.

Strangely enough, the Boy John letters came about almost by accident. He was already well-known to thousands of East Anglians who, for thirty years or more, had delighted in his homely rustic humour. Many more had heard him on the wireless for, although he resisted the blandishments towards the professional entertainment scene, the BBC had managed to cajole him into appearing before their microphones. But it was not until 1946, when he was in his late fifties, that his first letter was published in the *Eastern Daily Press*. Some time earlier, that friendly publication had expressed the wish that all its readers would enjoy a happy Christmas. Sidney, under the non-de-plume of The Boy John, decided to put pen to paper, and on January 2nd his letter to the editor was published. It began:

Dear Sar – Yow did print a message in yar pearper, a wishin all yar readers a happy Christmas. Well, me and Arnt Agatha, an granfar, thort as how we wud be sum o' the fust to rite an wish yow, an yar staff an orl, a werry happy New Year.

Arnt Agatha, she ha took yar pearper ever since that fust come inter our willage. Granfar he like them gays, wot yow have on yar front page. You had a good 'un a few months

Sidney Grapes

*back, that wus the picture of some cows a feedin on a green
with a pub at yin ind o the green. Arnt Agatha she liked the
cows, an I liked the willage green, an you can guess wot cort
granfar's eye.*

Thus began the saga of The Boy John, Granfar, Arnt Agatha
and the notorious Mrs. W– which was to delight the newspaper's
readers for the next twelve years. Both the editor and his readers
eagerly awaited each epistle, not knowing when it would arrive,
for Sidney refused all pleadings to make it a weekly feature. The
letters were very spasmodic in their appearance, for The Boy John
could only write when the spirit moved him. Indeed, during the
course of those twelve years the letters numbered barely a
hundred.

But each one was a classic, for they did not stem from the
imagination of a city gent attempting to portray the rural scene –
they came from a Norfolk heart and were true to the spirit and
character of the county. And the dialect was sheer delight. Like
most of us, he had difficulty in transferring the spoken words to
letters on a page and he frequently spelt the same word in different
ways, even in the same letter. But it mattered not one bit –
everything he wrote was the genuine article.

The last of The Boy John letters was sadly prophetic, though
nobody – except perhaps Sidney Grapes himself – realised it at
the time. It was written on April 7th, 1958, not long before the
Easter Fair on Tombland, and closed with the words:

*"Well, fare yer well, tergether. I sharn't see yer at
Tombland ter year".*

Exactly three weeks later, at the age of seventy, Sidney died.
For quite a long time he had battled against chronic ill-health, but
now there would be no more Boy John letters, and no more of the
philosophical sayings of Arnt Agatha which he had regularly
included as a postscript to the letters. The P.S. in that last letter
somehow seems to sum up the philosophy of Sidney Grapes:

*"Arnt Agatha, she say, 'Work is a cure for grumbling. Even
a mule can't kick when he's pulling' ".*

In contrast to Sidney Grapes there have been a number of men
who, over the years, have used the Norfolk dialect to great effect
as after-dinner speakers. Many of them were from the professions,
and it was my good fortune to enjoy a performance by one of

them while I was still just a teenager. The occasion was a rather posh affair and not one at which young lads would normally be present, but my father always took every opportunity of introducing me to the adult world which lay before me. Frequently, as he set off on one of his journalistic assignations, he would take me with him, having first tucked a couple of well-sharpened pencils into my breast pocket to give the impression that I was some young, aspiring cub reporter. I can recall interviews with such people as Sir Thomas Cook at Guist and the original Mr. Roy of Wroxham – and many other eye-opening expeditions. But the event in question was a celebratory dinner attended by almost everybody who had any kind of standing in both City and County.

Needless to say, my father and I did not attend the actual dinner – we made our entry as the dishes were being removed to the kitchen and secreted ourselves in a corner where my father could bring his shorthand into play and report on the speeches for the following morning's paper. I confess to having completely forgotten the identities of all the speakers except one. That man was Russell Colman, Lord Lieutenant of the County, High Steward of Great Yarmouth and highly acclaimed as the greatest Norfolk dialect exponent of his time. It was said that his repertoire of local stories and jokes was unsurpassed for both quantity and quality.

Norfolk humour was much more gentle in the twenties and thirties. It brought forth a warm chuckle rather than peals of laughter. It was slow and steady, reflecting the way they did things in the country in those days, and Russell Colman's humour was very much in that mould. Perhaps I may be forgiven for quoting just one, which reflects his connection with the fishing fraternity of Great Yarmouth – and perhaps I should explain to the uninitiated that a halyard is a rope for raising or lowering the sail of a ship.

The story concerned an old Yarmouth skipper who was selected by his colleagues to go to London and present a model of a fishing smack to Queen Victoria on behalf of the Mission To Deep Sea Fishermen. On his return, he made his report to his mates in the following words:

I went up to Buckin'ham Palace an' took that there model, and there was a feller what met me dressed like what you never saw, an' he say to me, "hev yew got that there model for the Queen?"

"Yis," I say to him. "That I hev".

"Well, then," he say. "Dew yew come along o' me then".
Well, bor, we went t'ru rume arter rume, an' at the finish
we come to a great curtain, an' he say, "Stand yew here, an'
when this here curtain is drawed to one side, dew yew go
in," he say.
Well, if yew believe me, I'd looked over that there model
a score o' times an' I hadn't never seen naathin wrong with
it. Then the curtain drawed open, an' there set the Queen,
an' I maade my obedience to har, an' I walked up, a-holdin'
of that there model. But, dew yew know what? Jest afore I
give it to Her Majesty I looked down, an' blow me if the peak
halyards worn't fast on the port side!
A gasp of disbelief came from his listeners.
"My heart alive!" said one of the men. "Whatever did the
Queen say to that lot?"
"The Queen?" said the old skipper. "She behaaved like a
perfect laady. She didn't pay noo regard".

In more recent times there have been three men who, in greatly
differing ways, have done much to preserve the Norfolk dialect
and, indeed, bring it to the attention of a wider audience. Briefly,
the trio consisted of a speaker, a folk singer and a poet, but each
one did much more than those bare titles would suggest.

The man who specialised in the spoken word was the late Dick
Bagnall-Oakeley. During his lifetime he became unquestionably
the greatest authority on East Anglian dialect of his time and,
though his normal manner of speech well befitted the academic,
gentlemanly Public School master that he was, he had the ability
to switch instantly into the Broad Norfolk that he loved. He had
made a lifelong study of the subject and was able to reproduce
every quirk of pronunciation, each little nuance of emphasis and
all the subtle changes of rhythm which made the dialect so unique.

He was always in great demand as a speaker to groups of people
all over the county, as well as a broadcaster and an adjudicator at
festivals of the spoken word. There are many people today who
remember Dick Bagnall-Oakeley with affection and, indeed, with
gratitude for the help and inspiration he gave them in their efforts
to speak "proper" Norfolk.

The contrast between the man of letters and the man of music
could not have been greater, for the latter was Allan Smethurst,
the Singing Postman. Allan of course, had a natural Norfolk

Allan Smethurst, the Singing Postman

accent; thick and authentic it was, for it was the only accent he knew. I recall the occasion, many years ago, when he told me that, like me, he was an Old Boy of the Paston School. How he managed to get through those four years without having at least some of the accent chipped away I shall never know. But, of course, it was part of him – he was born with it, and even cold steel would have made no impression on it.

Allan, helped by his accent and his wonderful sense of fun, made his name with recordings of his songs. Such local classics as *"Hev Yer Got A Light, Boy?"* and *"Hev the Bottom Dropped Out?"* were played all over the country and, even now, the few odd shillings in royalties still manage to find their way to him in his retirement home. But he was much more than just a singer of comic songs – the line of patter which held his act together was of the highest order. His great strength was as a live performer and his act had to be seen to be believed.

I well remember a performance he gave at the Central Hall in Wymondham some thirty or more years ago – indeed, how can I ever forget it? It was at the time when a well-known car construction company had uplifted its production line and entire workforce from their base in Hertfordshire and made a fresh start just outside Wymondham. There was to be a celebratory dinner, with local residents and newcomers getting together in a spirit of *entente cordiale*. My wife and I were invited to share a table with three directors and their ladies, and the Singing Postman was to provide the cabaret.

Now, the trouble was that Allan was sometimes a nervous starter, and such was the case that night. He was not very keen on taking the stage, and one of the organisers asked me if I would go and reason with him. I found him sitting despondently in his dressing room, his guitar by his side. Nervous tension had got the better of him, but I had taken with me a glass of alcoholic refreshment.

"Thanks, Bob," he said. "That orter help ter oil the warks".

I cannot recall the exact sequence of events in the next few minutes, but suddenly I found myself sitting by his side and singing a duet with him:

"Anno domini sixteen-six, as the tale was told to me,
Is a solemn date for us to fix
Deep in our memory..."

It was the Old School Song, and I suppose it was probably the only occasion on which that ancient Battle Cry has been rendered to the accompaniment of a single guitar. Then I almost pushed him towards the stage, promising him another pint when he had sung a couple of songs. He did as he was told, received a modest response from his audience and came back to claim his reward.

There then followed an interval of something like half an hour before he was due back on stage for his main act, and I then went backstage to check the situation. Now, I am not sure how many people had been helping him to "oil the warks" in those thirty minutes, but he was a changed man. His eyes were ever so slightly glazed, but the toothy smile and the spirit of fun had returned in full measure. He was ready to face his public and, for a full hour, he held them in the palm of his hand. At least, he held fifty per cent of them – the locals. I fear our newly-arrived friends were somewhat mystified by the whole affair, and I had a particularly arduous time with the directors and their ladies. They were nonplussed by Allan's patter, delivered in what must have sounded to them like a completely foreign language. They repeatedly asked me to explain his jokes. I did my best, but I am afraid they lost something in the translation, particularly in the case of one of the ladies who, it transpired, was of mainland European origin. I could do no more than assure them that they had, at least, had their first real dose of Broad Norfolk!

I went through into the bar, where Allan was busy signing copies of his recordings.

"What did the foreigners think of it?" he asked.

"They reckon they've never heard anything like it," I replied. It was quite true, though they had phrased their opinion in a slightly different manner. Then it was time for the Singing Postman to take his leave of Wymondham.

"Well, Cheerio tergether," came the familiar cry, and it was a happy man who shuffled across the car park and out into the night.

Finally, we come to the poet. The love of Norfolk folk for their native county has given rise to much more prose than poetry, for we are a cautious people, reserved, often hesitant in displaying our inner emotions. Even in prose it is not always easy to produce the rather flat, though sometimes undulating, rhythm of our speech which so reflects the very landscape in which we live. The ability to portray it in verse is possessed by very few. One man who, in my view, possesses that talent in abundance is John Kett.

John Kett

Writing in 1981 under the mantle of *Jonathan Mardle,* the late Eric Fowler said of him: "Of recent years, Norfolk has found in John Kett a writer who can capture in verse the rhythm, and the peculiar intonation and turn of phrase, of East Anglian dialect, and moreover express the homely sentiment and strong local patriotism of Norfolk people".

One cannot do other than think that the beauty of John Kett's verses stems largely from the fact that he is a complete man of Norfolk – even his name has a Norfolk ring about it! Like all his ancestors, he has lived his entire life in the county he loves, except for the six years when he was away at the War – and where should he be then but serving with the Royal Norfolk Regiment? He spent his working life schoolmastering, teaching Norfolk children in the Norfolk countryside. Now, in his retirement, his interests are all local and related to the Norfolk scene; still he delights in "the pattern of nature and its effect upon the countryside around us as the seasons come and go".

"I have tried to record something of my own enjoyment of the

Norfolk countryside in my verses," he said, "simply, as one is bound to do when using the Norfolk dialect with its limited vocabulary".

It is, I believe, his simple, unassuming approach to his wide diversity of subjects that gives John Kett's verses such charm. "The Broad Norfolk of John Kett," said Jonathan Mardle, "is the genuine article, and not the interpretation of a literary gent or the affectation of a 'foreigner' ".

I am grateful to John for allowing me to include one of his pieces. The choice was by no means an easy matter, and I have brought my natural bias into play in choosing one that reflects my love for the area of my birth.

POPPYLAND

That poppy growin' over there
Dew taake my mind back savrel year;
 That bit o' red
 That fill my head
Wi' memories o' Poppyland.

There in the cornfilds they looked fine
An' all along the railway line;
 We went that way
 On holiday,
Where poppies growed, at Overstrand.

There in't so many, bor, today –
They kill 'em orf wi' poison spray;
 But I recall
 Right well an' all
How good they looked in Poppyland.

CHAPTER 3

The Choice Is Yours

One of the inevitable results of the countryman's drift from the land and the consequent dilution of our dialect has been the near-loss of one of our best-loved rural institutions – the country story-tellers. They were men who, if one found favour in their eyes, could spin a yarn about almost any subject under the sun and who, no matter how fantastically unbelievable that yarn might be, could convince their listeners that every word of it was completely true. There are still a few such men among us, but they are very depleted in numbers compared with half a century ago.

The first of such men whom I encountered was Jacob. I suppose he must have had a surname, but I never heard it mentioned. Indeed, I think that, if a stranger to the area had asked one of the locals "Where does Mr. So-and-So live?" there would have been quite a lengthy pause before the reply came: "Oh, you mean Jacob".

It used to be said in those days that a true man of Norfolk lived with one foot on the land and the other in the sea. This, of course, was not a physical allusion, but rather an acknowledgement of the fact that, before the advent of mechanisation and industrialisation, they were the two elements around which the lives of Norfolk people revolved.

With Jacob, however, it was doubly true, for he spent six months of every year on each. From early spring until the harvest had been gathered in, he tilled, sowed and reaped the fruits of the soil. Then he would take himself off to sea as a deckhand on one of the boats that chased the shoals of herring down from northern Scotland to our east coast ports. He never claimed to be a sailor, for he had no great knowledge of the sea. He was welcomed on board solely for the strength of his body, a vital attribute for hauling in the herring-filled nets before the introduction of mechanical aids for that particular task.

The shoals of herring were vast in those days and the combined Scots and English fleets of drifters numbered several thousand. More than a thousand of the boats were registered at Yarmouth alone, and each September their numbers were swelled by twice

Landing fish at Yarmouth in Jacob's time, c.1900

as many Scottish boats. Yet, strange as it may seem, the herring stocks withstood that amount of fishing, for it was before the introduction of steam-powered boats and the greed that came with them. In Jacob's time the drifters ploughed their way down the coast with only the power of the wind in their sails to carry them on their journey. It was a tough life for the men who brought in the harvest of the sea – and Jacob was as tough as any.

I have little idea of how old Jacob was when I first met him. I was with Jack, my schoolfriend, and we were about nine or ten, for it was in that glorious age when children could roam the countryside at will, safe in the knowledge that no harm would befall them. At that age, of course, anybody over thirty was "getting on a bit" but, though Jacob was officially retired, he was still active and ready to give a helping hand to anybody who needed it. It would be only partially correct to say that he lived in a little stone cottage hidden away a mile or so from the town. That was, indeed, his home, but he was an outdoor man.

"I never could bear to bide indoors," he said. "Mind you, there have been mornings when I looked at the sky and wished I could lie abed till dinnertime".

The fact that he never did was borne out by his complexion – as near mahogany as one could ever imagine, and with a pair of arms of the same shade of brown and as solid as the strongest timber. At times he was called upon to dig a grave for some parishioner who had departed this life.

"I can't say as how I enjoy it," he said. "Thass what you might call a labour of love. You see, I knew him – dear old boy he was – and his missus, too. Anyway, somebody have to do the job. Someone 'll have to be a-doin' it for me afore long".

When Jack and I were engaged in our wanderings in that area, we usually knew where to find him. There was a gap in one of the hedgerows where presumably there had once been a gate, and there he would be, wearing his old fisherman's gansey, looking across the fields in the direction of Bacton and the sea. It was there that we would sit, looking for all the world like the figures in Sir John Millais' painting of *The Boyhood of Raleigh,* while he told us tales of the past. It was he who told us the true story of Old Shuck, the dog of peace that pounds the roads looking for its lost master – far removed from the picture painted by modern writers who seem to get him confused with the black hound of Odin and the black dog of Bungay.

He told us many tales of people and places all over the world; tales of strange happenings and fantastic creatures that stirred our boyish blood – but, were they true stories? Of course they were! We had heard them from Jacob!

I never knew what happened to Jacob in the end, but I know he went to his grave a happy man, for he spent his life in the open air doing the things that he wanted to do. He had chosen the path which he had trodden, and he would have chosen it again. He was a member of that happy band of men for whom W.H. Davies prophesied the greatest inheritance of all:

> *When will it come, that golden time,*
> *When every heart must sing?*
> *The power to choose the work we love*
> *Makes every man a king.*

It was from another of Norfolk's old story-tellers that I heard the tale of Charlie Gates and his Yellow Car. I prefer not to name my informant but, having been closely associated with him for very many years, I can vouch for his integrity in these matters. Admittedly, I have never heard him make the definitive claim that his story is true in every detail, but I like to think that it may well be so. Anyway, let me tell you about Charlie and his car.

The story is set in the 1950s, and Charlie was a farmer. His was only a small farm – one of the many such holdings which still existed at that time before they started linking them together to make way for the bigger equipment. He also had an old motor car which used to take him around the farm and into the town. It stood as high as a horse, and his men claimed it was ten times more trouble; they always said that a horse could have got things done more quickly than the car, but it was Charlie's pride and joy. In those days, when nearly all cars were black, it may seem strange that he should have painted his such a vivid shade of yellow, but he had a perfectly logical reason for so doing – he had just enough paint left over after he had finished painting his binder, and he was never one to be wasteful.

One day he had an appointment in Norwich at 1 o'clock but, as he also wanted to pick up some day-old chicks from somewhere near Dereham, he thought it would be a good idea to kill two birds with one stone by going round that way. Accordingly, he collected his chicks and then made his way to Dereham to get on to the Norwich Road. Everything was going according to plan but, just as he got through Dereham, he came to a road junction, and there he had to stop and wait while a convoy of circus wagons and caravans went past. There he sat, patiently waiting for the long procession to go by until, right at the end, there was a young lad leading a rather large elephant.

It was at this point that Charlie's troubles began for, as it got on to the crossroads, the elephant took one look at the bright yellow car, pulled itself away from the young lad, ambled across, turned round and sat down on the bonnet of the car. Now, an elephant sitting on the bonnet of a car is not really to be recommended, and the result was that Charlie's car suffered quite a bit of damage. There was a rather large dent, a collection of scratches, and one lamp was left hanging loose. Charlie, quite understandably, was none too pleased by the occurrence and complained in no uncertain manner to the circus men. They, for their part, were quite nice about it – most apologetic, in fact. But, they said, it was really Charlie's own fault. At this, Charlie saw red.

"My fault!" he exploded. "How can it be my fault?"

"It's your fault for painting your car bright yellow," said the circus owner. "You see, our elephant is trained to sit on a bright yellow tub in the circus ring – it's all part of his performance – and, when he saw your car, he thought he had got to go into his act".

Charlie was not pleased, to say the least, but time was getting away and he wanted to get to Norwich for his appointment. The circus procession moved off and Charlie started the yellow car on its way, one headlamp still dangling loosely from the side of the bonnet. Then he spotted a roadside garage some distance ahead and decided to pull in and ask what they could do to repair the damage.

"Well," said the mechanic. "We can't do much today, but we'll have a look and see what it's likely to cost".

Standing conveniently next to the garage was a public house and, seeing this, Charlie suddenly felt thirsty.

"Well, dew yew be havin' a look," he said. "I'm just a-gorn' to pop in there for a drink".

He stayed just long enough to imbibe a couple of pints and, realising that he was now in danger of being late for his appointment, he climbed into his car and proceeded in the direction of Norwich. He soon had the little car running at full speed and, by the time he came to the first set of traffic lights on the outskirts of the city, she was bowling along quite merrily.

Now, Charlie maintained that those traffic lights were green, but the constable who stopped him on the other side said they were red. In spite of this disagreement, I think Charlie might have got away with it if he hadn't talked so much, but it wasn't long before the constable smelt his breath.

"Have you been drinking?" he said.

"I only had a couple on the way," replied Charlie. "Don't hang about – I've got this appointment at one o'clock. I'm late already and I want to get on".

The policeman, however, realised he was on to something and, as policemen do at such times, he began to wander round the car as if on a tour of inspection. Needless to say, he soon saw the large dent, the chipped paint and the lamp hanging loose.

"Hello, hello, what have we here?" he said. "How did this happen?"

Charlie looked him straight in the face and said innocently, "An old elephant came and sat on it just outside Dereham".

Not surprisingly, the constable didn't believe him. Nor did the magistrates when he came up before them some days later. He was fined £20 for being drunk in charge of a car.

Even then, however, his troubles were not over – there was more to come. The circus people took him to court for spoiling their show. It seems that the elephant was no longer willing to put his hindquarters on anything yellow since he scorched his bottom sitting on Charlie's bonnet. Charlie had to pay another £20 so that they could train it to sit on a different-coloured tub.

A true story? Or complete fabrication? The choice is yours. It may not be completely convincing on the printed page, but if you could hear the story-teller's voice and see his "butter wouldn't melt in my mouth" expression I think you might be hesitant in making your decision.

Another of our well-remembered story-tellers was Walter Henry Barrett, usually known as Jack because in his early years, we are told, he resembled an uncle of that name. Jack was a real Fen Tiger, living much of his early life in the Feltwell Fens where, he said, "From Brandon Creek to Hockwold cum Wilton there weren't a firm groundsel to place your feet on, the whole weary miles".

Freedom and liberty ruled the lives of the old fenmen, and it was these old characters who dominated most of his writings, although his later life in South Norfolk opened up new fields of human behaviour for him to explore. His stories were always well-researched and based on the people and places he had known throughout his life – they were not mere hearsay.

His first book, *Tales from the Fens,* did not achieve publication until he had passed his seventy-second birthday, but he soon made up for lost time with *More Tales from the Fens* and *A Fenman's Story.* Sadly in 1974 and at the age of 83, Jack died, leaving another unfinished manuscript on which he had been working. All his labour was not wasted, however, for, at the request of Jack's widow, his close friend Percy Garrod took over completion of the work and in 1976 *East Anglian Folklore* completed a splendid quartet of local volumes.

Strangely enough, however, the story I have chosen to include is neither about the old fenmen, nor was he able to vouch for its authenticity, for it is a light-hearted piece which he acquired almost by accident. It was written in pencil on an age-stained piece of paper amongst a collection of odds and ends which an elderly man had given him some sixty years ago.

The story concerned a genteel Norfolk lady – a lady of title, no less – who had been treated by her doctor over a long period of time after having suffered a nervous breakdown. Progress was slow but steady, and eventually she reached the stage at which the doctor considered that she would benefit by something other than the conventional treatment he was giving her. In short, she needed a long holiday away from the routine of her daily life. He went so far as to recommend a certain German village at the foot of a range of mountains.

"Three months there and you'll be a new woman," he said.

The patient agreed to the doctor's suggestion, but she had one or two slight problems to overcome before she could make the trip. She had never travelled abroad; she had no knowledge of the German language; and it was before the time of travel agents in every High Street. Then she had a brainwave. There must be a school in the area, she thought, and it was possible that the teacher might speak English. She would write.

She wrote her letter; there WAS a school; and the schoolteacher had a fair command of English. All the arrangements were made, but then the titled lady, so fastidious by nature, realised that she had omitted one vital question – that of toilet arrangements. She had failed to ask if there was a W.C. attached to the house where she was to stay. Such a facility was absolutely essential, so she hurriedly wrote another letter to the teacher asking for particulars as to the W.C.

Unfortunately the teacher, though having a reasonable knowledge of English, had never encountered those initials and had no idea of their meaning. After much thought, however, inspiration struck. He knew the lady to be of strong religious persuasion, so the answer was obvious – she wanted to know where the Wesleyan Church was situated.

A few days later the Norfolk lady received his reply:

Your Ladyship,

The W.C. is situated about seven miles from your Ladyship's lodgings in the centre of a pine forest amidst lovely surroundings and is open on Tuesdays, Thursdays and Fridays. This is rather unfortunate if you are in the habit of going regularly, but you will be pleased to know that a number of people take their lunch there and make a day of it.

As there are many visitors during the summer I would advise you to go early.

The accommodation of the W.C. is excellent and there are eighty seats. The bell will ring before the W.C. opens.

I strongly advise you to pay a visit on Thursday as there is an organ accompaniment. The acoustics of the W.C. are excellent and the most delicate sounds are audible.

I should be delighted to reserve the best seat for your Ladyship and have the honour to sit with you.

Yours -----

A true story? Or is it fiction? Once again, the choice is yours.

CHAPTER 4

The Penny School.

During the first half of the nineteenth century, entertainment for the masses in eastern England was provided by a chain of theatres owned and run by the renowned Fisher family. They were mainly situated in market towns, and bands of entertainers would travel from one to another with all their scenery, props and costumes packed into various forms of horse-drawn transport. As one such group left one of the theatres, the next one was already on its way to take its place, thus offering an ever-changing programme of entertainment.

Fisher's Theatre in North Walsham first opened its doors to an incredulous public in 1828. Its Vicarage Street exterior gave little indication of the wonderland which lay within for, if contemporary prints are to be believed, both stage and auditorium offered facilities which must surely have been the envy of many a larger town. Indeed, one wonders whether Mr. Fisher was, perhaps, slightly over-ambitious in providing such a theatre, with seating for several hundred people, for a community which, at the time, numbered little more than two and a half thousand. Anyway, whatever success he may have anticipated was destined to be short-lived and, by 1841, his theatre, having fallen into disuse, was offered for sale.

Failure for Mr. Fisher, however, brought a heaven-sent opportunity to certain other members of the local populace.

For a long time there had been a feeling that some form of education should be provided for the increasing number of children in the town, and this was too good a chance to be missed. Thus it was that, in 1842, the former theatre became transformed into the National School, which was run on a voluntary basis until 1870.

Then, the Elementary Education Act decreed that "the parent of every child not less than 5 years of age, nor more than 13 years of age, shall cause such child to attend school". The following year saw the election of a School Board, who decided that the fee for each child should be one penny per week (hence 'Penny

Fisher's Theatre,
North Walsham, 1828

Schools'), together with the stipulation that the children must provide their own stationery.

Thus, in 1872, the Board School came officially into being, with Mr. Edward Snell in charge of the boys and Miss M.A. Escott looking after the girls. The extra influx of children must have made things somewhat difficult for these two worthy teachers, but somehow they soldiered on under the one roof, with nothing more than a curtain to separate them. One can only wonder at the standard of education they were able to provide, particularly when, after two years, the school register contained the names of no less than 400 children. Drastic measures were then necessary and, accordingly, local builder Mr. R. Cornish was called upon to erect a new building at Marshgate, where it still stands as part of the enlarged establishment which now caters for the educational needs of the younger generation.

When the children were transferred to these new premises their numbers had increased to 500, of whom a hundred were segregated to form the Infant School under Miss Sarah Lander. This helped to ease the state of congestion which had earlier developed, but it still meant that there were only three qualified teachers to mould the future lives of five hundred children. To make matters worse, it was found that the standard of stationery being provided by the pupils was not satisfactory, so the weekly fee for each child was increased to twopence, with the School Board supplying the necessary materials.

The new building was set among fields in those early days and, as many of the children had to walk several miles across open country, attendance depended very much on the weather. An entry in the School Log for July 25th, 1874, reported that "Unfavourable weather has been an impediment to regular attendance". There were also other reasons for absence. On August 31st we find the note: "Attendance very poor when school re-opened because many were still gleaning", whilst the entry for October 29th states that "Several were absent acorn gathering". It is interesting to compare these entries with one in the Log of Cromer School for October 5th, 1883, which states: "Attendance very poor this week. On Friday there were 90 children absent, 40 of whom were infants under 7, to pick up coal from a wreck".

The early School Logs make fascinating reading, for they give a factual account of what life was like for both the children themselves and the men and women in whose care they spent their days. Discipline was enforced in a variety of ways, and one can only feel sympathy for a young girl named Nellie whose misdemeanour and subsequent punishment were recorded in the entry for December 5th, 1910: "She persisted in being noisy in the corridor after one or two warnings from me. I therefore caned her on the left hand and, in order to prevent her cries disturbing other classes, I locked her in the girls' lavatory. I took the precaution of locking the door to prevent her from running home. At 11-15 a.m. the girl's mother came to the school, having been informed by a child of her daughter's detention. The mother stated her intention of complaining to the Managers and, finding that the girl's underclothing was wet, took her home to change her clothes. I therefore cancelled the girl's attendance in the register".

Poor little Nellie!

There was little in the way of formal teacher training in those early days and, even if such qualified people had been available, it is doubtful if the Board were in a position to pay the salaries which such staff would have expected. Hence it became necessary for the three worthy teachers to select and train children from their own classes, thus bringing into being the once-familiar system of Pupil Teachers. This, of course, is now a relic of the past but, at that time, as well as providing a source of much-needed cheap labour, it was also the only way in which a child without well-to-do parents could enter the profession.

Promising boys and girls were recruited by the time they had reached the school-leaving age of thirteen, and sometimes even as young as eight or nine. They then became known as Monitors or Monitoresses for a period of time during which their aptitude could be assessed. Most of them received no pay at this time, although some received one shilling per week. During this period many, for a variety of reasons, fell by the wayside. Some were found to be unsuitable; others were withdrawn by their parents, who saw a better future for them in work on the land or in service; and others gave up for medical reasons. Among the latter was Jessie Snell, daughter of the boys' headmaster, who was advised to give up any ideas about teaching because of her weak health. In due course she married Arthur Loveless, a local grocer who also had a jam and fruit preserving factory in Hall Lane. One cannot help wondering, however, whether she would have benefitted from a second opinion, for she led a full and active life and succeeded in passing her hundredth birthday.

Hilda Rump.
(see next page)

The next stage for those children who were accepted was that, for the following twelve months, they became known as Candidates. Then they were subjected to examinations, success in which enabled them to reach the giddy heights of Pupil Teachers. This signalled the start of a formal apprenticeship which lasted for a further five years, during which training went on in earnest. They were required to take charge of a class during the day and to further their own studies in whatever time was left after preparing lessons and marking their charges' work. Throughout those five years they were subjected to frequent examinations and inspections, and only then would come successful qualification – and a salary in the region of ten shillings per week.

It was quite a contrast with the professional training of teachers nowadays, and there are those who might claim that such a long association with one particular school, from early childhood onwards, must inevitably lead to a certain narrowness of outlook. The people of North Walsham, however, can readily refute that argument by recalling the name of one person who passed through the system and went on to earn the undying love and respect of countless children who passed through her hands. She was Hilda Rump, who became a pupil in 1899, a monitoress in 1907 and then a qualified teacher until her retirement in 1960 – an unbroken span of 61 years at the same school. At the same time, she took evening classes in shorthand and secretarial duties in both North Walsham and Cromer, and engaged in a host of other activities – even to the extent of becoming an expert archer!

Over the years, Hilda Rump became not just a small-town teacher but rather a pillar of the local community, greatly respected and much-loved. She lived with her sister in their little house on the Aylsham Road; Hilda was the breadwinner and her sister the housekeeper. On Sunday mornings they were a familiar sight as, clad in their tweed suits with twin-sets and pearls, they made their way to and from the Parish Church. Hilda, indeed, usually sported a pair of ear-rings from the large collection which was her pride and joy.

Opposite Page: Staff of North Walsham Council School, early 1930s.
From left to right, <u>*Front Row:*</u> Miss Rump, Miss Gow, Miss Wiles,
Mr. & Mrs. Colthorpe, Miss Mace, Miss Wenn. <u>*Middle Row:*</u> Mrs. Taylor,
Miss Pattle, Miss Thompson, Mrs. Brundle, Miss Savage, Miss Spelman,
Miss England. <u>*Back Row:*</u> Miss Page, Mr. Howell, Mr. Allen, Mr. Anstis,
Mr. Childerstone, ? Miss Hunter.

My first meeting with Miss Rump came in 1925, when I found myself starting my academic career in the "Mixed Infants". It was a year when the school was visited by His Majesty's Inspectors and, though the occasion meant nothing to me at the time, I eagerly feasted my eyes on their report when a copy came into my possession a year or two ago.

"The type of child attending the school," said the Report, "is somewhat mixed. There are several groups of delicate and backward children, some of whom are inherently dull, but the teachers endeavour to give them work suited to their capacity and attainments, and encourage them to use what ability they possess. The brighter children are making good use of their opportunities".

Where, I wonder, did I figure in the Inspectors' portrait of our school?

During my years at the school, the teaching staff numbered a score or so, most of whom were unmarried ladies. Of the men, there are several who, for greatly varying reasons, stay in my memory. I recall the headmaster, Mr. Colthorpe, mainly for his unfailing belief that corporal punishment was the cure for all ills. Then there were Mr. Howell, Mr. Newson and Mr. Anstis. 'Snag' Anstis had the unsettling habit of standing behind a pupil to inspect his work and then, if what he saw gave him displeasure, bringing his hand up and giving the boy a sharp cuff across the ear. Rumour had it that an injury during the Great War had left him with one hand completely devoid of feeling, and we thought it rather unfair that this was the hand he used to inflict punishment.

Of all the male teachers, however, I remember Harry Allen with the greatest affection and gratitude, for it was he who first kindled in me a love of the English language which has never left me.

Among the ladies there was Miss Florence Gow, headmistress of the Infants' School, who sent me a letter of sympathy and a little box of sweets when a sudden attack of mumps prevented me from playing the part of Humpty Dumpty in the annual concert.

There was Miss Dennis, young, pretty and – though she played in goal for a local hockey team – so kind and gentle. It was for that dear lady that I suffered, for the first time, the pain and anguish of unrequited love – and I was six years old at the time!

And then, of course, there was Miss Rump. Hilda was a character – and she knew it! North Walsham was the poorer for her passing.

2

Country Matters

Give fools their wealth
And knaves their power,
Let fortunes bubble and fall.
Who sows a field, or trains a flower,
Or plants a tree, is more than all.

John Greenleaf Whittier.

CHAPTER 5

Saving The Stanford Harvest

If one drives out of Thetford on the A134 towards Swaffham or the A1075 in the direction of Watton, one is treated to a splendid vista of typical Breckland landscape. Unfortunately, however, the rugged beauty of the scene can only be admired from afar, for the area fringed by those roads constitutes what most people know as the Battle Area. The Army prefer to call it the Stanford Training Area or simply, in typically official jargon, "Stanta".

It was in May 1942 that the Army commandeered those 26 square miles of Breckland, and the takeover was carried out with unseemly haste. If they had to have a training area in East Anglia where they could use live ammunition, then I suppose the parishes around Stanford were probably the best choice, as there was much wild heathland which had always been considered of too poor a quality to merit cultivation. But there were about a dozen farms in the area, many cottages, a small private school, public houses and churches. Above all, there were the five villages which were to be sacrificed to the demands of War – Stanford itself, Tottington, Sturston, Langford and Buckenham Tofts. And what of the people who lived and farmed there? They were given notice to leave their homes, taking with them their livestock and all their worldly possessions – refugees in their own homeland.

The War Agricultural Committee tried to stop the takeover, stressing the amount of food which would be lost, but they were fighting a losing battle. So the Committee set about the task of helping the evacuees – finding them new farms, new jobs, new accommodation. They were promised that they would be able to return at the end of the war, but that promise was never honoured and now, half a century later, the Battle Area is still there.

When the last of the evacuees had been moved out and the Army had taken possession, there remained yet one more problem to worry the War Agricultural Committee – the standing crops, of which there were some 3,000 acres of corn and 1,000 acres of sugar beet and other roots. It seemed wrong to abandon all that food, and they managed to persuade the Army to stop training for a fortnight in August and a fortnight in October so that the crops could be harvested. John Mann was put in charge of the operation, but most of the responsibility for organising the project fell upon the District Officer, Dr. H.G. Hudson.

Harold Hudson was well-known in the area, both for his farming knowledge and his organisational ability. The whole operation required very detailed planning in advance, for they were told that they could not enter the Area before the beginning of each fortnight, and that the Army would recommence training – with live ammunition – immediately the fortnight was over. Hence, they surveyed the area before the Army closed it, locating each field which had to be harvested.

Fortunately, the Committee had a number of tractors and combines, but time was so short and valuable that they had to be sure that, if any of the machinery broke down, repairs could be carried out with no delay. Thus, they set up a field repair workshop and made arrangements with local agricultural engineers to give priority to any major repairs which might be necessary. They would need fuel, so they took over a garage and arranged for petrol to be available every day. Fortunately, the combines were 'sackers', so they did not have to transport the grain in bulk, but they did have to lay in a store of sacks. Then there remained just one more problem. The tractors pulling the combines had to be driven and, although the Committee had a few men, they were not enough, and it was not feasible to rely on neighbouring farmers, for they were busy with their own harvest.

Harold Hudson solved the problem by appealing to his old school, Repton, to send a party of senior boys. They responded nobly by sending 20 boys in the care of two masters, who did a magnificent job. Major Maynard, who had been Harold's form master in the Upper Sixth, was in charge and volunteered to run the garage and petrol pumps. They took over the school as an office and hostel, and they found a housekeeper. They had to have a manager to arrange for the corn to be collected and sold, and a secretary to deal with the paper work. They persuaded Mick Sanderson, who lived and farmed just outside the Area at Bodney, to take on the first job; and Edna Kerridge from East Harling took on the secretarial duties.

They all had to be ready to move into the Area at 6 o'clock on the first day of the fortnight so, on the previous day, they assembled the combines, the tractors, the fuel trailers, etc., just outside the boundary. The boys arrived from Repton, the housekeeper assembled her stores, and supplies of fuel were at the ready. They already knew where each field of wheat and barley was situated and had planned which to cut first.

Then, at six o'clock precisely, they moved in – the combines to their allotted fields; the boys to the school to dump their kitbags and move out to their jobs as arranged; the housekeeper and her helpers to unpack their stores and organise the hostel. The boys from Repton drove the tractors pulling the combines; they sacked the corn off, humped the sacks and had the time of their lives. Major Maynard ran the garage with military precision and was covered in grease and dirt by the end of each day. Mick Sanderson took samples of corn to the local merchants, sold it and arranged for it to be collected. They learned as they went along. They made mistakes and worked flat out from dawn to dusk. Then, by the end of the fourteenth day, they had completed their task; every crop had been harvested and every piece of equipment had been moved out of the Area.

They caught the public imagination, and the Press descended upon them and got in the way. The glossy weeklies heard about the Repton contingent, came and photographed them, and wrote them up in the *Tatler!*

During the fortnight there was just one major catastrophe, for which Harold Hudson accepted full responsibility. He had left his wife at home with their four-month-old daughter and, as bombs were dropping on Norwich on most nights, she was becoming increasingly nervous. Harold suggested that she might like to move in with them and possibly help with the catering and cooking. This she did, and she arrived complete with the baby and their pet dog, a Cairn Terrier named Timmy. What they did not know was that the housekeeper had also brought her dog – a prize pedigree Pekingese. Unfortunately, the two dogs met. Even more unfortunately, the Pekingese was a bitch and Timmy was not. They became friendly. The housekeeper was not amused.

Six weeks later they went back again to harvest the sugar beet and mangolds. This proved to be much more difficult. In those days, the process of lifting sugar beet had not been mechanised, and each root had to be pulled, knocked and topped, and loaded by hand. The Repton boys were not available, but the Army offered help in the form of 900 soldiers, who set up camp just outside the Area.

The organisation was far more complicated. The soldiers had to lift and knock – they were excused from topping, for the danger that soldiers would cut off their fingers was too great. The Army provided lorries, took the beet to railheads outside the Area and loaded them into trucks to take them to the factories.

Once again, harvesting had to be completed in fourteen days and, as before, they finished on time. But there was a different feeling about it. The corn harvest had been one big party; they enjoyed it and were sorry when it was over. But the sugar beet harvest was one long slog, and they were glad when it was finished. In August they had been helped by the Repton boys, who entered into the spirit of the thing, worked hard, and enjoyed every minute; in October they had the Army, who thought it was a dirty, boring chore, grumbled all the time and couldn't wait to get back to training and fighting. But it was a memorable, if hectic, interlude.

Today, the Battle Area is still under military occupation and firmly closed to trespassers, although the Army is very co-operative in welcoming organised parties of visitors by prior arrangement. Those who were thrown out in 1942 were never allowed to return, and the promises that were made in such haste were quickly forgotten.

One day in November, 1992, not many months before his death, Harold and I sat mardling over coffee and dredging up mutual reminiscences. It was, I suppose, inevitable that the Battle Area should figure in our memories and, although Harold was in no way involved in those broken promises, I could not fail to detect a feeling of remorse in his recollection of the events of 1942. Yet we both agreed that the Army's occupation of the Area had brought an unexpected legacy, for Stanta has become a nature reserve. The fields are no longer ploughed, and only occasionally are they grazed by sheep, and the whole Area has reverted to its natural state. It has become a sanctuary for birds and other wildlife which seem unperturbed by explosions and military movements. It is more than half a century since those who lived there were evicted, and the old bitterness has died. Now we have come to realise that the farmers' loss has become the conservationists' gain, and that we have inherited, by pure chance, an area of supreme ecological importance.

"But," said Harold, "I still feel sad at being associated with a solemn promise which was never kept".

CHAPTER 6

Miss Reeve of Tottington

It is not easy for the outsider to imagine the state of turmoil that existed in the Breckland villages of Stanford, Tottington, Sturston, Langford and Buckenham Tofts when, in 1942, the inhabitants were ordered out of their homes to make way for the forces of war. Urgency was the order of the day, and no amount of impassioned pleading or protests at public meetings could bring about a change of heart by the military authorities; those 26 square miles were vital to the successful prosecution of the war. Everything and everybody had to go – and quickly.

There was, of course, the assurance that they could all return once the war had been won, and the optimists among the population consoled themselves with the traditional belief that it would be "all over by Christmas". There were a few who, having struggled to make a living from the unforgiving Breckland soil, looked forward to more kindly-disposed conditions wherever they might eventually find themselves. For most, however, it was a question of meek subservience as the trail of refugees, with their livestock and worldly belongings, made their way to different destinations outside the designated boundary of the area.

Subservience, however, was not a word that figured in the dictionary of Miss Reeve, for she was a fighter.

Lucilla Reeve was born at Tottington on March 28th, 1889, and, right from the outset, she carried a handicap which was to haunt her throughout her life – that of having been born out of wedlock. Nowadays, of course, few people would give the matter a second thought, but it was a great social stigma in Lucilla's time and many people were quick to remind her of her doubtful parentage.

One cannot help thinking that Miss Reeve was a born loser but, having said that, one has to add that she won more battles than she lost. She was born to the land and rapidly developed a deep affection for her native Breckland and, in particular, her beloved Tottington. Once, in her childhood, she stayed for a while near Dedham, which had been described to her as one of the most beautiful villages in Constable country.

"To me," she said, "my village is far more lovely".

By the time she reached womanhood she had developed great resilience and strength – two characteristics which were to come to her aid many times in her adult life. She was something like 5 feet 9 inches in height and sturdily built, with a full, roundish face which at no time ever bore so much as a dab of paint or powder. She wore her long, black hair sensibly swept back and tightly clipped in place. She could not be described as a pretty woman, nor was she ugly – just plain. She knew that young male suitors were unlikely to beat a path to her door, but this was of no concern to her. She was tough and strong-willed – not the sort of woman who would be willing to play second fiddle to a husband, which was, after all, the accepted role of many of her contemporaries. Her only interest in the male sex lay in their ability to work – and she prided herself on being able to work as hard, and as fast, as any man in Breckland.

Her normal working clothes were businesslike and sensible – a dark blue or black jacket and skirt with matching pullover, and a white starched blouse buttoned up to the neck. Then, to complete the ensemble, there were thick lisle stockings and a stout pair of brogues. When engaged in the more physical side of her work, the skirt gave way to a pair of corduroys tucked into long woollen stockings.

She was an accomplished horsewoman and could handle a gun – and she was equally at ease with the Lord of the Manor or the farm labourer. Hence, it was really no surprise when she became Agent to the owner of the Merton estate, Lord Walsingham. Even with her employer, however, she was never one to mince her words; her opinions, once stated, were strongly defended. She took particular exception to the amount of time and money spent on rearing game birds to provide sport for about a month in the year. Much better, she believed, to use those resources to improve harvest yields and help to feed the nation. Such views, not surprisingly, did not endear her to her employer.

She was something of a mystery to the villagers, for they were unable to fit her into any of the conventional categories which governed their lives. She had reached a position of authority while still a young woman, which in itself was unusual at that time. Yet they knew her to have been born to a working class mother, with no recorded father. Certainly, she could dig ditches and handle farm machinery in a working class manner, yet she was known to have artistic and literary talents, for her writings regularly appeared in the *Eastern Daily Press* and *The Farmers' Weekly*. Nor was this the sum total of her activities, for she was also an experienced dowser – and in their eyes the whole business of divining the source of water smacked strongly of witchcraft. Then there was her belief in ghosts – she claimed to have seen several and had written about them. Finally, there was the day when she was accused of being a follower of Sir Oswald Mosley, simply because she attended one of his meetings to find out what it was all about. No, Miss Reeve never really fitted in, and thus she tended to become something of a loner.

In 1938, eight of the farms owned by the estate had to be let, but farming was in a depressed state and Miss Reeve's task was not easy. Eventually, however, she found tenants for seven of them, leaving just Bagmore Farm at Stanford. But Bagmore Farm was rundown and derelict. Nobody wanted it. It was then that Miss Reeve made one of the greatest decisions of her life – she would take it on herself.

Her friends were horrified. "What, that old place!" they said. "You must be MAD!" She would never get anything to grow, they said, and even if she did it would be eaten by the hordes of rabbits which infested the land.

Then there was the fact that she had insufficient cash to buy the necessary farming equipment, but she soon found an answer to that problem – she would open her house as a guest house! Needless to say, it was not a great success. In her first year she welcomed just one single guest, together with a group of four who were the overflow from a large shooting party up at the Hall.

"Yes," said her friends. "She's mad – quite, quite MAD!" But she wasn't really mad – she just believed in miracles and, as readers of her book, *The Earth No Longer Bare,* will recall, she created her own miracle at Bagmore Farm.

Working for the most part with basic implements and minimal assistance, she brought order out of chaos. To a bare and unproductive land she gave fertility. She soon discovered pigs to be a paying proposition, for they made a profit and, at the same time, enriched the land. Portable sties could be used on rough ground, and the pig manure, together with her clover leys, built up further acres for cultivation. She tried sheep, cattle and even goats, but her greatest success was probably with her ducks at Eastmere. All the while, as if her crops and livestock were not

Miss Reeve's ducks at Eastmere.

sufficient, she carried on a continuous afforestation programme, planting thousands of trees and changing the very face of her little bit of Breckland.

But then, in 1942, came the bombshell. Miss Reeve was not a superstitious person – after all, her most productive field was her 13-acre – but it was on Friday, June 13th that she was told that her farm was required for military purposes. Everybody in that group of Breckland villages was given notice to quit, with the promise that they could return after the war.

That night, as she confided in her diary, she wept solidly for hours until sleep eventually overcame her. When she awoke, she was filled with a feeling of inner calm, and her mind was made up. She would refuse to go!

The military authorities were incapable of understanding Miss Reeve's attitude to her environment. Was she just an awkward, stupidly recalcitrant woman? She was a Norfolk woman – she made that quite clear. She would go through hell and high water to keep her land. To her, it was not just a matter of pounds, shillings and pence. It was her land, her life, her heritage. She refused to budge.

The men of war were not pleased. Their patience was fast running out. They issued an ultimatum, giving her two choices. Either she must leave, like the rest of the evacuees, or she could stay in her house but give up the land. Still she elected to stay. And stay she did!

Then, one evening, her telephone rang and, quite out of the blue, she was offered employment in another part of the county. A certain estate needed a Land Agent. There was a house with all modern conveniences, an office with staff, and 3,000 acres to look after. At first Miss Reeve thought it was a joke but she checked the details and found it was genuine enough. The workings of Miss Reeve's mind, however, were known only to herself. The new post might well be in Norfolk, but it was not in her beloved Breckland. She declined the offer.

She continued to live in her house at Bagmore, but it was not long before the sight of the tanks churning up her fields and knocking down barns and outbuildings became more than she could bear. She knew that she would have to leave. But where in Breckland could she go? The solution was one that only she could have dreamed up. She managed to acquire three wooden chicken huts and a tin garage, and these she installed just outside the northern boundary of the Battle Area, not far from Merton. Then followed a succession of trips in her little car, transporting all her worldly belongings to her new settlement, and there she proposed to live and wait for the end of the war. As she made her final trip, with her car tightly packed with her last possessions, and her two ever-faithful dogs in the back, she took one last look back over Spring Breck. Later that evening, she sat down and put her emotions into words:

The Tanks are out on Frogshill Heath,
My Clover ground to dust beneath
The wheels of war; I see the wreck
Of hay and corn, across Spring Breck.
And mighty men of war stood there,
To watch the Tanks sweep through my corn;
They did not care, they did not care,
And only I was there to mourn.

I drove my car down Frogshall Hill,
The hour was late, the earth was still;
The trees look'd down with pitying eye,
To see the laden car go by.
My heart was sad and bowed my neck,
Four years of work and planning wreck,
Behind me lay, across Spring Breck.

Despite her somewhat rugged exterior, Miss Reeve had a heart which overflowed with love – but, apart from her two dogs, there was almost nobody with whom she could share it. Above all, she was the greatest of all patriots, with an undying affection for her King and Queen, for whom she was in the habit of writing verse on special occasions. She loved Breckland and, in particular, her native Tottington and its people. Every year, as Armistice Day approached, she remembered seeing the young men of her village going off to the First World War in 1914, many of them never to return. Then she recalled the time when she helped to raise the money to build a simple memorial to the men of whom they were so proud.

They had organised splendid cricket matches which went on all day, with the added attraction of stalls selling sweets, cockles and gingerbread. They sold teas, soft drinks, vegetables, fruit and flowers – "and the winning team capped round, and the losing team were fined!" They had hoped, rather ambitiously, to raise sufficient money to build a small almshouse for a war widow, but they had to settle for a plain stone memorial to the men who had died in what they had hoped was the war to end all wars.

Then there was the battle with an all-powerful vicar, who insisted that the memorial should be in the form of a tablet on the wall of the church. They pointed out that many of those men were Non-conformists, and their relatives and friends had helped to raise the money. Surely it was only right that the memorial should be in the centre of the village, where they could lay flowers or say a prayer. It was a Sunday in 1919 when it was unveiled – after much delay because they could not get anyone to take the service.

All these thoughts went through Miss Reeve's mind on Remembrance Day in 1945 as she mounted her bicycle and set off to a service of Remembrance such as she had never expected to attend. It was at Tottington and, on her return, she confided to her diary the day's happenings:

There were no crowds at my service. No clergy walked at the head of a congregation singing hymns, with children carrying flowers for the beloved dead. No birds sang in the trees, and no cattle stood in the meadows. The dead and staring eyes of the cottage windows, where once the geraniums bloomed and the spotless curtains fluttered, looked out on a scene of desolation. The sides of the once tidy main road were full of holes made by tanks roaring through on their way to train for war; and the once lovely hedges of privet, lilac, thorn and wild roses were mangled and torn. A silence as of night brooded over all.

The hour was eleven, of this eleventh day of the eleventh month, and my heart was full as I whispered a few words of thanks to those who had made the great sacrifice in those far-off days. I was able to put my few flowers through the surrounding railings and say a prayer for all peoples of the world, and nobody said me nay, for I was alone.

She cycled on to see the ruins of what had once been her home, gutted by fire following shelling by tanks in the previous year. The pine trees and the shrubs had grown so much that they almost hid the ruin from view until she reached the gateway. She was beyond tears as she walked round the one wall which still stood. Strangely, the garage was undamaged, and she noticed the two holes, one large and one small, which she had cut in the door for the swallows to get to their nest inside. She had made two holes, forgetting that the young birds could have used the parent birds' hole.

"It is the little things of life we so often remember in our darkest hours," she wrote. "And, going up the meadow on my return, I thought of the day when, cutting the blackthorn hedge in the orchard, a thorn had gone deep into my hand. It never came out, and I used to be told, to tease me, that a sloe bush would grow out of me when I was dead – and I had said what a pity it couldn't be a proper tree".

Then, back once more in the wooden huts which had been her home for the past three years and were destined to be still her home for several more, she looked across the village to the woods in their autumn glory.

"It was a lovely sunset," she wrote, "and did we not say 'At the going down of the sun we will remember them'?"

So the years passed and Miss Reeve patiently waited for the chance to return to Bagmore Farm. As each year went by, however, she began to feel more and more the effects of the physical and nervous strain she had undergone, and she wondered whether she would be capable of starting all over again. Then, with the coming of 1950, she had reached the age of 61, and she knew in her heart of hearts that she could never again face the torments of the past. It was then that she hatched another of her plans.

Tottington Church

Some time earlier she had seen a vacant house "in a north-easterly village, a few miles from two coastal towns, and overlooking 13 acres of water". It was true that it was not in Breckland, but living there would be somewhat better than her seven years of life in converted poultry huts and a tin garage. Furthermore, there was room there for a family of three besides her – and she knew of just such a family. She had been promised a farm equivalent to Bagmore. Surely it would be cheaper for the authorities to buy this house and re-house two families from the Battle Area at once.

But No – the people in power considered it unseemly for folk to profit from war, so the costings would be calculated on pre-war prices. There was no chance whatsoever of acquiring the house.

Lucilla Reeve had been a fighter all her life, but this was the last straw. On Armistice Day in 1950, when most people were remembering the dead and reflecting upon the futility of war, she took her own life.

The clergy did, at least, respect her wish that she should be buried in her beloved Tottington. Not for her, however, were there the blessings normally bestowed upon the dead, with the sure and certain promise of eternal life. The priests laid her body to rest in a piece of unconsecrated ground just outside the churchyard – outside salvation.

But that was not the end of the story, for Fate can play some strange tricks. At some time in the next year or two, part of the boundary fence around Tottington churchyard collapsed. Whether it was storm damage or the result of being knocked down by a tank is a matter for speculation, but I rather suspect the latter, for the military decided to rebuild it. They started off by following the original line of the fence, but then they came to an area, something like 9 feet by 20, where there was obviously a grave. They decided that the grave must be included in the churchyard, so they extended the fence around that area and linked up with the original line on the other side.

Some time ago I spent a lovely summer's evening in the Battle Area as a member of a coach party led by the Commanding Officer. Every now and again the coach would stop so that we could climb out and inspect something of interest, and one such stop was at Tottington Church. There, I hung back as everybody else went inside the church and, when they came out, they wondered why I had not joined them. But I was elsewhere. I had gone for a stroll around the perimeter of the churchyard, and there, near the mound of grass and rubble that was once the old rectory, was Miss Reeve's grave. I stood and looked, smiling inwardly and thinking to myself:

"Well done, old girl – you beat 'em in the end".

Farmer George Raby of White House Farm, Thornage, sends
his workers and their families off on one of the annual trips
to the seaside which he organised, early 1900s.

The Preston brothers, renowned Holt photographers,
out for a family trip to the coast. Tom Preston is
by the rear wheel and "Chummy" sits beside
the driver, Ben Empson, c.1909.

The Back sisters of Hethersett
had their own unique form of transport.

Ling's Garage at Holt, with two open-topped cars
suitably adorned for some special occasion, c.1908.

61

CHAPTER 7

Two Men and Their Dog.

Life in the country in the earlier years of the century had much to recommend it, but it also brought hardship, especially for those whose livelihood came from the land. Without today's mechanisation, such tasks as lifting and topping root crops or harvesting frost-encrusted sprouts were nobody's idea of fun. Without motorised transport, even the transfer of livestock from farm to saleground was not without its problems.

Ben Burgess retains vivid memories, as a young man in the 1920s, of driving a flock of five hundred lambs from the family farm at Howe to Clement Gaze's Saleground at Diss – a distance of 21 miles – with just one other man and a dog to help him.

"It's all very well," says Ben, "to conjure up a picture of the shepherd at the head of the flock with his faithful dog following behind. Such was, perhaps, possible when moving a flock from field to field, but I have yet to hear of a dog which would clear a way through sheep or cattle for an overtaking motor car or shut an open field gate. No," says Ben. "The road to Diss necessitated two drovers in addition to the dog".

By tradition, Diss Lamb Sale was always held on the first Thursday in July, reasonably near the longest day of the year so that, by 3-30 on the Wednesday morning, there was sufficient light to start the 21-mile drove. Initial progress, however, was slow. A flock of lambs fresh off their mothers had no desire to run away. On the road they just wanted to get into a huddle and, if they covered a mile in the first hour, the drovers thought they were doing well. It was not long, however, before the lambs recovered their appetites and began to graze on the roadside verges. The verges of the 1920s were very different from those we know today. The continued passage of grazing cattle and sheep ensured an ideal sward for the lambs – indeed, they preferred it to their home pastures. Thus the pattern was set. The search for fresh grazing produced a movement of lambs from the flock, up the middle of the road to the front, where the stream divided right and left in the quest for new grass. Gradually their speed increased as hungry lambs got the hang of it. Soon, the ones at the rear would run a hundred yards or so up the middle of the road to continue their meal. From then onwards, the drovers' job mainly consisted of interrupting the grazing of the rearmost lambs.

Although the amount of traffic in those days was minimal when compared with that of today, one cannot help wondering how the drivers of vehicles reacted when suddenly confronted with such a large flock on the road. But it was all done according to an established system. The horse traffic or occasional motor car which wanted to overtake caused no inconvenience at all. It simply joined the stream of lambs running to the head of the flock. Traffic meeting the flock caused slightly more trouble and, when the drovers saw traffic ahead, they were obliged to stop urging the rear lambs forward until the whole centre of the road was clear.

With the prospect of 21 miles to travel during daylight hours, it was not unnatural that they took the very shortest route, bearing in mind that very narrow roads with narrow verges slowed up their progress, whilst the wide Ipswich Road from Long Stratton to Burston allowed them to make good progress in spite of the increased traffic.

Today, it is not easy to visualise the entire route from Howe to Diss virtually without a single gap in the hedgerows. In an age when almost all livestock was driven along the roads, however, it was in every farmer's interest to maintain stock-proof roadside hedges. Thus, the only temptation for driven animals to stray from the intended route was at a road junction or by the occasional field gate left open. Incidentally, it was never necessary for the man in front to stand in a side road until the whole flock had passed; once a few score of sheep had gone forward in the right direction it was very rare for one to be so independent as to wish to explore the side road.

Ben's journey with his flock took them by way of Scott's Pasture, south of Shotesham, to Bussey's Loke. They avoided Hempnall Street, taking instead the Tasburgh road for a few hundred yards before turning left over a ford. Here they lingered for a while, for, if their charges did not take advantage of this supply of water, they might not get another chance to drink until they got to Diss. From the ford they crossed the main road going west from Hempnall and so to Fritton Common. From there they took a right turn towards Morningthorpe, passing several hundred yards of unfenced roadside which sometimes caused problems.

Lamb Sale at Diss, 1918.

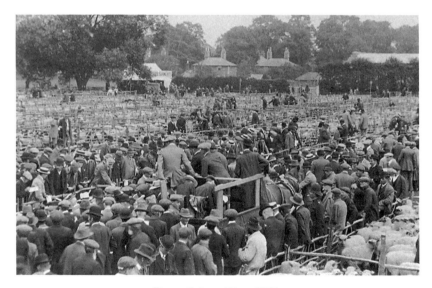

Sheep Sale at Diss, 1913.

Then they made for the Ipswich Road, just south of Long Stratton Street at the church turning.

"Sometimes today," says Ben, "as I now drive from Stratton to the Burston turn just short of Dickleburgh at my legal 60 m.p.h., I think of those long drives along the same stretch with 500 tiring lambs. The drivers of what few cars there were treated us in the most friendly fashion and expressed their gratitude for our help. Perhaps they recognised our ancient right to use the road".

It was along this stretch of road that they became aware of other flocks of lambs, both in front and behind, also on their way to Diss. All these flocks had to find a temporary resting place within a mile of the Saleground before dark. Ben's contingent were lucky and privileged, for Clement Gaze allowed them to lie on a small pasture on his Brewery Farm, only a few hundred yards from the Saleground.

The nearest route to this favoured venue necessitated their turning right off the main road at the bottom of the hill approaching Dickleburgh and passing in front of the Burston Strike School, then newly built and the centre of much Trade Union activity. On one occasion their passage past the School coincided with the end of a meeting at which one of the Pankhurst sisters had been expounding her beliefs. "She was most friendly," says Ben.

Further on, through Diss Heywood or maybe Shelfanger, they cut off a corner by proceeding straight forward through a wide green lane, probably as much as a mile long. It was there that they came across a score or more of local lads playing quoits for high stakes. The choice of site for this illegal pursuit was a good one, for the lane was some twenty or thirty yards wide and an approaching policeman could be spotted from as much as a couple of hundred yards.

From the end of the green lane it was but a short distance to the flock's nocturnal resting place at Brewery Farm. Then, having got the lambs on the meadow, there was just time for Ben and his colleague to walk into Diss for a pint and a sandwich before returning to a sound night's sleep in the deep straw of a Brewery Farm loose box.

On two occasions in the early 1920s Ben Burgess found himself driving sheep in the opposite direction to that which he had taken with his lambs. He was at the July Ewe Sale in Diss to buy replacement shearling ewes, in each case numbering no more than forty or fifty. He could, of course, have driven them to Diss station, loaded them up for Trowse and then driven them home from there to Howe. Driving them home through the night, however, held no fears for him and, although he was alone and without a dog, that is what he did on both occasions. And he is the first to admit that each of the droves taught him a salutary lesson!

On the first occasion he bought the lot of ewes which best suited his eye and his pocket – but he neglected to take into account the distance they had already been driven to the sale! He only discovered his mistake when they were out on the road – they were already tired and footsore from the flint roads on the previous day's journey. By the time they reached Pulham Workhouse and the Queen's Head Public House, which was beside it on the road, his spirits were as low as his sheep's legs were weary. There was no moon, but fortunately there were no other sheep in the little enclosure beside the Queen's Head. Ben was just in time to have a drink and a much-needed piece of cheese before closing time. He paid the landlord the half-crown demanded by him for the use of the enclosure, and he promised to be on his way by first light.

"And," says Ben, "I don't think I ever slept more soundly than I did that night on a heap of roadman's shingle beside the gate into the lairage. If there was any traffic on the Ipswich Road that night, I didn't hear it!"

When he awoke, his little flock was rested and enjoying an early breakfast on the tempting short grass of the lairage. He left them to feed a little longer than he had agreed with the landlord – but he was not to know! It was very slow progress during that day, and there were times when Ben began to think of another night on the road. His ewes were so footsore that he hadn't the heart to push them along, but in the end they made it – and he had learned his lesson.

The following year, Ben's choice of sheep to buy was perhaps unduly influenced by the condition of their feet. This time they went past the Queen's Head at a steady two miles an hour. Although it was dark when they turned off the main road, there was no danger of anybody running into them, for he had an eighteen-penny flashlight to warn any driver of a motor car or horse and cart which happened to be on the road.

It was well past midnight and, approaching Fritton Common at

One man and his dog – and a bicycle for the return trip!
Billy Wright of Sharrington, shepherd to Sir Dymoke White, driving his flock through Stody.

a steady speed, Ben had every hope of getting home by breakfast time. Then, unfortunately, one of his little flock got herself caught up with a large bramble left on the roadside by an idle hedge-cutter. It took Ben several minutes to disentangle the ewe from the bramble, after which they both went forward at an increased speed to catch up with the rest of the flock.

"Then," says Ben, "imagine my surprise – one hundred yards, two hundred, three hundred and no sign of the sheep on the road. Then I realised that I had also lost the ewe with the bramble. I found there was still a hedge on the left and an open common on the right. Mild panic set in – I had lost my little flock on Fritton Common. Even in broad daylight forty sheep could be lost there amongst the bushes and furze.

Ben spent half an hour amongst the thorn bushes, but all to no avail, so he gave up the search and looked around for a friendly stone heap. There was none. He decided that, in daylight, he could easily follow the tracks of forty ewes however far they had strayed. He sat down with his back against a gatepost; it was most uncomfortable, but eventually he dozed off.

Some time later, on waking up, he found that he was sitting in a thick mist – the last straw, he thought; how could he possibly find his sheep in those conditions? He was cold and stiff, so he decided that he could at least go for a brisk walk on the road to get his circulation going. He stood up and, lo and behold, his head was above the mist, and the bushes on the common were floating as on a dead calm sea.

He walked back towards Morningthorpe to where the common began and took a few steps on the common, thinking that, when the mist lifted, he would find his sheep. But he had no need to go searching, for there at his feet were forty shearling ewes in a compass of as many feet. They seemed not the least surprised to see him, neither did they bother to get to their feet. They had just flopped down on reaching the common, grateful for the rest. He dared not risk disturbing them – he dreaded to think what might happen if, refreshed, they had gone off to graze in the mist.

Of course, all bad things, like the good ones, come to an end. Within an hour the mist had lifted sufficiently for them to continue their journey. They reached home just before one o'clock. Nobody seemed surprised to see them – "We thought you'd be home by lunchtime," they said.

CHAPTER 8

A Sharp Ol' Frorst.

I have a strong feeling that, were it not for the vagaries of our weather, many among us would be hard-pressed to find a subject for everyday conversation. A movement of a few degrees up or down the thermometer; a Siberian breeze scudding across the cliffs at Cromer; a sudden peal of thunder on an otherwise Spring-like day – all are topics for immediate discussion. I think it must be because of our climate's changeable nature, for I cannot imagine eskimos, nor the heat-soaked natives of equatorial Africa, stopping to talk about their weather. Yet, from surprisingly early times, the English have been recording weather conditions, particularly in relation to severe winters.

The earliest I have yet come across relates to the year 359 when, it is recorded, the winter was so severe that the sea was frozen all round the coast, and every river was transformed into solid ice. The intense frost lasted without a break for nine weeks.

There were many similar reports in succeeding years, and then, in 1281, winter struck in a manner which surely would have tested the endurance of today's centrally-heated generation – and it made its attack with a double-edged sword. "From Christ Mass until Candle Mass," we are told, "there was such fierceness of frost and snow here in England such as no man living could remember from before nor ever wished to behold again". Then, with the thaw, even greater calamity was to come: "Great was the woe in our land then. Good people were swept away and drowned, scores at a time. Five arches of old London Bridge went with this flood, all of Rochester's fine bridge, and hundreds like of needed bridges all over England".

When it came to a question of snow, surely the winter of 1615 must rival any other in the recorded history of England. It started to fall on January 5th and continued at intervals every day and night until March 12th. The whole land became a vast snowfield; every town, village and road was obliterated. "And many hundreds – nay thousands – perished under this vast white shroud, so fearsome were the hardships caused by it".

People found their way about by 'remarking and remembering' the tops of the tallest trees and, when it was all over, wise men in the lonely moorlands set about planting long lines of pines to mark tracks between homesteads and roads.

In 1683 came 'The Great Frost', still believed by many to have been the most severe this country has ever known. It persisted for thirteen weeks without a break. Oaks and other hardwood trees were split to the core; softwood trees were killed outright; and the sea was frozen some miles out from the shore. John Evelyn, the diarist, noted its effects and recorded them for posterity:

1683 – Dec 23rd – The Thames frozen, it being in England one of the severest frosts that has happened for many years.

1684 – Jan 1st – The weather continuing intolerably severe, the air so very cold and thick, as of many years there has not been the like.

Jan 6th – The Thames quite frozen.

Jan 9th – I went across the Thames on ice.

Jan 16th – The Thames was filled with people. On the Thames there were booths and formal streets, shops furnished with commodities, a printing press, coaches plying in the streets, horse and coach races – all on the ice.

And so on, well into February.

In 1709 came a frost that, in Norfolk, killed old people in their beds and wiped out almost all the wild animals and birds. It froze milk solid as it came from the cow. "At that time," it is recorded, "the cold without was like a separate living thing, ready to slay if it could but strike you".

In 1827 the Thames was again frozen, and oxen were roasted on the ice. In Norfolk similar conditions existed and, though I have no knowledge of ox-roasting in these parts, the townsfolk of Diss made good use of the ice, even to the extent of playing a cricket match on it! The story was told as follows in the *Norfolk Chronicle* of March 10th, 1827:

The continuance of the frost having occasioned that fine piece of water – Diss Mere – containing above five acres – to be safely frozen over, the 20th of February was fixed for playing a match at cricket on the ice, which commenced at 10 in the forenoon, and was well contested all that day, concluding about 6 in the evening. There was also ten-pins, running, skating, sparring and every other kind of appropriate rustic sports. Stalls and booths were erected to supply all kinds of refreshments. At one, a card party sat till past 10 at night. No accident occurred though it was computed that more than 1500 persons were present in the course of the day.

Diss Mere on that occasion must have presented a wonderful spectacle. I have never seen it in the grip of ice, but at all times it is a unique feature of the town. Indeed, the two are inseparable, and the late Eric Pursehouse, renowned local historian and headmaster of Diss Grammar School until his retirement in 1959, said, "The Mere is Diss; Diss is the Mere". Certainly, social life and local occupations have always centred around it, and the town even takes its name from the Mere, for Dice (or Disce) was the Saxon word for a pool of standing water.

Many years ago it was considered to be bottomless and, rather fancifully, to have been formed in the crater of an extinct volcano. Whatever its origin, it is known to extend to some 5¹/₂ acres and to have a maximum depth of twenty feet. It is served by a number of underground springs, and Eric Pursehouse described how, when swimming in the Mere, he could feel the current of these springs coming up underneath him.

Because of the continuous movement of water above these springs, such ice as would form in that area was always thin and unreliable, and it was the custom to place upturned barrels there to warn skaters of the danger. Even then, the strength of the ice had to be tested before skating and other activities could begin, and we are told that, in 1827, such testing was carried out by a Mr. Clarke of Stuston, who "drove a cumbersome farm wagon, drawn by four heavy horses, and crossed from one side to the other without mishap".

During the early part of the First World War, the ice was sufficiently thick to enable a moonlit dance to be held on it, complete with a piano to provide the music. On this occasion the ice was tested by two intrepid (or, perhaps, foolhardy) gentlemen who drove across it on a motor cycle and sidecar.

One winter in the early 1930s, when there was sufficient frost to provide a few days of skating, the occasion was marked by the appearance of a lady skater clad in Victorian dress, with cloak, muff and bonnet reminiscent of the 1890s. "Though without practice for some years," we are told, "she sailed round gracefully with perfect balance and technique and her hands in the muff. But she was no novice – she had learned the art in the nursery of champions, the Fenlands".

But one of the greatest freeze-ups of all time must have been in the winter of 1890/91, when skating took place on the Mere for some thirteen weeks. It was truly Eskimo weather, with heavy snowfalls to go with the ice. A Watton man, Mr. G.C. Green, took his young bride to a farmhouse in Suffolk on November 26th; the snow started to fall on that very day, and the ground and roads were not seen again until the middle of March. Dare I suggest, perhaps, the longest honeymoon on record?

Not surprisingly, the people of Diss were quick to take advantage of the conditions, and skating on the Mere started on Boxing Day, 1890. By the following Saturday, January 3rd, the ice was safe enough for the 30-strong Rifle Band to play a programme of music in the middle of the Mere. This was so successful that arrangements were made for "A Grand Carnival and Fancy Dress Fete (Jack Frost permitting)" to take place on the following Saturday. There were, however, those who feared that there might be a sudden thaw to frustrate their carefully planned scheme. Hence, these enthusiasts decided to hold a similar event on the previous Thursday and, though hastily improvised, the event was crowned with success.

Picture the scene. I quote: "At 9 p.m. the flares from a host of torches, fixed in the barrels and arranged in a huge circle, lit up the arena. In the centre, another ring of gently swaying Chinese lanterns enclosed the Rifle Band. High spirits prevailed and the profusion of colourful fancy costumes of the skaters – Father Christmas, Ally Sloper (see Chapter 19), Bogey Man, Buffalo Bill, Harlequin and a host of others carrying Roman candles – transformed the Mere into a fairyland. Feathery flakes of gently falling snow enhanced the general effect". The proceedings terminated at 10.30 p.m. with a procession of skaters round the fringe of the Mere, with some 2,000 persons witnessing or participating in it.

The prime object of the carnival arranged for the following Saturday was to raise funds for the relief of the distressed, for many workers had been laid off because of the weather and there was no unemployment pay. Contemporary accounts record "the air of gaiety about the town, the masses of bunting, and the spirit of carnival which increased as the numerous visitors, with their skates, arrived by rail and road from distant places such as Ipswich and Woodbridge, in all not fewer than 5,000".

"A selected band of persuasive ladies and gentlemen wearing

A skater's delight as Diss Mere freezes over, 1907.

distinguishing sashes wove skilfully in and out among spectators and reaped a considerable harvest for the needy. At dusk, a fire balloon was released which, at a good height, discharged brilliant lights over the closing stages of the carnival".

Another similar event was planned for later in the month but, on that very morning, a rapid thaw set in, covering the ice with a film of water. The evening programme had to be abandoned and, though a balloon was released, it was whisked away and "its brilliant spectacle was lost to Diss". But there was a torchlight procession through the town, led by the Rifle Band, and "with many merrymakers in fancy dress delighting the jostling crowds in the Market Place. A memorable day ended with the National Anthem and the orderly dispersal of the spectators".

During the more recent past Norfolk has known spells of severe wintry weather, but very few of them could stir the populace to the kind of activity enjoyed by those worthy folk of Diss. There have been many winters within living memory when we have had a few days of heavy snowfall bringing chaos on the roads and cutting off towns and villages, but many of these were isolated cases during an otherwise normal winter. There are, perhaps, just a handful which have challenged those of earlier times.

There was the winter of 1928/29, though I was little more than a fledgling at the time and well protected in the family nest. But George Jessup, a valued friend and highly respected chronicler of Breckland matters, is slightly my senior and remembers it well. It was a winter marked by the worst excesses of frost and snow, and he recalls skating on Loch Neaton at Watton from December 8th to March 30th.

On one Sunday during that period, George was at Scoulton Mere when 'Happy' Tofts and Roy Cook of Hingham drove a car on the ice all round the Mere, a feat repeated a week later by Colin McLaren of Watton.

1947 was the year when we probably had more snow in Norfolk than at any other time in living memory, for the ground was never clear of it from Christmas until the beginning of the following April. The night of March 10th/11th saw the heaviest fall, with up to 20 inches on the level and drifting to as much as 20 feet. The combination of heavy snow and severe frost was disastrous to wildlife and, being a naturalist, George particularly remembers the loss of thousands of local birds – notably bearded tits, snipe, kingfishers, bitterns, woodcock and wrens.

The winters of 1958 and 1963 must still remain in the memory because of the severe combination of frost and snow, with motor vehicles abandoned, power supplies cut off and helicopters being used to take emergency cases to hospital. But it was 1944 which holds a special place in George's memory, for it really was a white Christmas – but without any snow! Hoar frost spread over the land on Christmas Eve, and by Boxing Day the whole countryside presented a picture of breathtaking beauty, when even unsightly things like barbed wire were transformed into objects of fairy-like charm. George and his wife went for an 8-mile walk on the afternoon of Boxing Day – "to Merton and through the Park, and everywhere one looked it was the most wonderful picture that we had ever seen. We have seen many excellent ones since, but none that quite rivalled that one".

Nowadays, pampered as we are in our centrally-heated homes, frost and snow mean little more than inconvenience, with cars abandoned, power lines brought down and Norwich city centre grinding to a halt. Never again will Father Christmas, Ally Sloper and Buffalo Bill glide beneath the Chinese lanterns in time with the music of the Rifle Band on Diss Mere. And never again will Mr. Clarke of Stuston be called upon to take his four-in-hand across to test the ice.

3

Men of Business

If each before his own door swept,
Then all the street were clean.

Sir George White.

CHAPTER 9

Rumsey Wells – Capmaker.

Everybody, we are told, loves a bargain. Certainly the almost indecent haste with which the January Sales begin – long before most of us have disposed of the Christmas turkey – gives credence to that belief, and shopkeepers make the most of it. Signs proclaiming "Bargains in all Departments" and "Prices Slashed" bring in the crowds like pilgrims on their way to Mecca.

Yet there was, in Norwich, a purveyor of clothing to whom such methods of advertising would have been complete anathema. The last thing Herbert Rumsey Wells took into consideration was cheapness – his only objective was quality. His great speciality was headgear, and he rightly claimed that one of his meticulously-made caps would outlive three or four of the cheaper specimens available elsewhere – and would be more comfortable into the bargain. It was with pride that he advertised himself as "The Most Expensive Capmaker in the World".

Rumsey was the fourth in a family line of capmakers which had come into being with his great grandfather's rather genteel announcement in the *Norfolk Mercury* on March 4th, 1815. "George and Samuel Wells, of 14 Cockey Lane," it said, "beg to acquaint their Friends and the Public that they have this day opened the above situation, where there is now ready for their inspection an elegant and extensive Selection of Goods, in all its various branches". Later, about 1849, the firm was joined by the next generation in the form of Thomas Wells, and then, around 1870, by his son, also named Thomas. In 1899 a move was made to No.6, St. Andrew's Street, and seven years later, with business expanding, they transferred next door to No.4, which they leased from Lacon's, the brewers.

In 1905, Herbert Rumsey Wells – the son of Thomas Wells Junior – became a partner in the firm, which then traded as T.Wells & Son. Rumsey was not long in making his mark and, a century after his great grandfather had inserted that first polite announcement in the *Norfolk Mercury,* he addressed his public rather more forcibly.

"Some men," he wrote, "wear some sort of a cap made from some sort of cloth, cut in some sort of way – the sort of chap you see in railway carriages (God forbid they should be seen anywhere else) – they serve their purpose there, I suppose, but, if these men knew what awful sights they looked in them, they would have more respect for themselves and consideration for those who have to look at them".

When George and Samuel Wells first opened their business in 1815 only a small minority of members of the male population wore caps. Schoolboys wore skimpily-cut affairs, but adults, even when engaging in such activities as golf and cricket, favoured the tall beaver hats which were a symbol of the times. Gradually, however, the fashion changed and the larger, more comfortable and better-fitting caps which the Wells' were producing steadily gained in popularity. But it was Rumsey who put the jewel in the Wells' crown with his inspired creation – the "Doggie" cap. Each Doggie was individually made to conform with measurements of the prospective wearer's head. These measurements, taken with a piece of equipment known as a conformateur, were then recorded in order that any customer, however distant he might be, could order another cap to be sent to any corner of the globe, safe in the knowledge that it would be a perfect fit. Rumsey claimed, indeed, to be the only capmaker in the world to cut the peak of a cap to conform to the shape of the wearer's forehead.

He had agents in many overseas countries and he claimed that his customers were recognised throughout the Empire by fellow ex-patriots who, with a hearty handshake, would greet them with, "I don't know who the blazes you are, sir, but you're wearing a Rumsey Wells cap, so dash it, come and have a drink!"

The standard Doggie was priced at a guinea, though there were other variations which, made to suit specific needs, could cost as much as two pounds. They were made, he said, of "the nicest English, Scotch and Irish tweeds, sewn with English sewing silk, lined with English Polonnaise silk, and made in the capital of the King's County, Norfolk". Each variation had its specific name – there were the 'Blofield', the 'Brancaster' and the 'Brundall', brought out in steady succession rather like the new motor car models of the present day. Indeed, there was a Doggie specially made for motorists – the 'Reepham', which protected the back of the head from draughts and was guaranteed to stay in place even when motoring in a sixty-mile-an-hour gale!

Herbert Rumsey Wells, "the most expensive capmaker in the world", 1933.

Rumsey always made it known that he would at all times welcome comments and suggestions from his customers, and this brought a response in the heatwave of 1933, when golfers complained that the 'Blofield' was too hot and heavy for the conditions. His reaction was immediate. He produced the 'Westwick', made from open-mesh linen instead of tweed and tipping the scales at a mere $3^1/2$ ounces. The customers were duly impressed.

Younger members of the public were also catered for, and generations of Norfolk schoolboys have memories of being supplied with the 'Lad's Sprowston' for as little as 6s.6d. Nor did Rumsey forget the ladies. "A lady's cap," he said, "is something entirely different in every respect from the creation of the milliner for, while the latter is worn on occasions and is sheltered from sun and rain, the cap is for all weathers and every day – in fact, to live in". He produced ladies' caps in a variety of materials, but it was the slightly baggy 'Rumishanter', with its matching scarf, which really caught the mood of the twenties – and all for half a guinea.

Herbert Rumsey Wells was one of the real characters of Norwich, and a jolly one at that! I think it could also be said that he, himself, was the best advertisement for his business. He was a dapper little man, with his slightly rotund frame clothed in tweed suiting and, very often, wrapped in an Inverness Cape. In his earlier years he sported a monocle, but my memory is of his twinkling eyes shining through thin-rimmed spectacles, his ever-neat moustache and his short, tidily trimmed goatee beard. And on his head, of course, there was inevitably one of his own creations – a Doggie Cap.

As a younger man, he was often to be seen making his way through the city with arms bent and chest thrust forward over the handlebars of his bicycle. Indeed, he was, in his day, one of the most renowned of local racing cyclists on the track and, in his maturity, he played a major part in attracting the top continental champions to come over and take part in cycling events in Norwich.

I suppose it was inevitable that Rumsey and his shop should have always seemed to have so much in common. There was the man himself – artist, traditionalist, and so very, very English – and the shop, which reflected the lack of change in the business during the one and a half centuries of its existence. The premises, neatly tucked in between the Shrub House public house on one side and Theodore Salkind's antique business on the other, clung to the atmosphere of a house rather than a shop, yet it was packed with the Wells specialities of "head-gear, neckware and legware" – and much more besides. There were, of course, hats and caps in a wide variety of styles, together with scarves, neckties and badges in every conceivable club, school or regimental design. There were glass-fronted mahogany cupboards and display cases packed with cuff-links, tie-pins and a host of other accessories. And there were those splendid blue, canvas-covered boxes with brass handles which were so intriguing to my childish mind. What, I wondered, could they contain?

Another feature of the shop which captured my boyhood imagination was something which previously I had only seen on cigarette cards. It was a collection of military headgear of earlier years which had been lovingly collected by the Wells family. They were fascinating objects, each with not only a proud history but also a strong local connection. The very names of the regiments conjured up visions of brave deeds in past wars: The Norfolk Yeoman Cavalry, The City of Norwich Volunteers, Hay Gurney's Light Horse, The West Norfolk Militia and, finally, a regiment often quartered in the city in the mid-nineteenth century, The Sixteenth Lancers.

Rumsey's affection for past traditions also led him into a revival of one of the city's formerly-thriving industries – weaving. It was in 1916 that he sought out a few of the experienced weavers left in Norwich and proceeded to turn out finely-woven silks in a variety of traditional patterns. He managed to uncover an 18th-century peacock-patterned Norwich design, which he proceeded to offer to the public in no less than five hundred colourings. Success was immediate, and he was not slow to inform the public that "the attempt to revive the Norwich silk industry has received Royal recognition" and that his company "has been honoured with Royal Commands for His Majesty The King, His Royal Highness The Prince of Wales, and other members of the Royal Family".

Meanwhile, the more soberly-coloured silks were being used to supply Rumsey's clerical customers with vestments of Norwich silk, which seems rather appropriate when one recalls that, at one time, the half-mile length of St. Andrew's Street boasted no fewer than seven churches.

Rumsey Wells was a great lover of tradition, and no story of his business would be complete without mention of the crest which he himself designed soon after joining the family business. I suppose it could be more correctly called a rebus for, while the lower half portrayed three wells to represent the three generations of the family which had preceded him, these were surmounted by a rising sun, symbolising his entry into the trade. The crest figured on all their stationery and was depicted, in more tangible form, on the large shield which greeted customers as they entered the shop.

It was in 1920 that the flamboyant Rumsey had taken over control of the business from his father and, for the rest of his days, he and his shop occupied a unique place in the life of the city of Norwich. I suppose there were some to whom the shop was a little bit "posh", but it was also rather special, as was its owner. But it had to end; nothing lasts for ever. In December 1937, at the age of 60, Rumsey died – and there was no fifth generation to take his place. It seemed like the end of a tradition.

The staff, however, had other ideas. They refused to accept the prospect of such a splendid organisation fading into oblivion and, in consultation with Rumsey's widow, they formed the business into a limited company. The Company Secretary was Mrs. Edna Watling, who had joined the firm as secretary in 1929 and was known to many customers simply as "the elegant lady in Rumsey Wells' ". Also on the Board was Mrs. Elsie Bugden, who had joined the company on leaving school, and the two ladies proceeded to guide the business through the years until it finally closed in 1974. For some time it had been difficult to find suitably skilled craftsmen and, when the lease of the premises expired, the door was finally locked on almost 160 years of history.

"It was a wrench," said Edna. "It was my life's work". She could have sold the Rumsey Wells patent, for she had a number of tempting offers, but when it became apparent that potential buyers wanted to go in for mass production, Edna said "No". She wanted the name to be forever associated with individual quality and fine workmanship – not shoddy imitations.

She and Elsie Bugden still look wistfully back on their years in that unique little business in St. Andrew's Street, and they have their memories. They recall the men who would visit George Everett in Dove Street to have a plus four suit made to measure for £3-10s. and who would then take a piece of the cloth to Rumsey Wells for a matching Doggie Cap at a guinea or so. There

The Rumsey Wells Rebus and the Doggie Cap Trademark.

was the American airman who disliked his Service hat and spent the last war flying from Norfolk wearing a specially-made Rumsey Wells forage cap. And there was George King, the Hingham steam enthusiast, who bought his Doggie for his son's wedding and then habitually wore it when driving his 1917 Garrett steam tractor to rallies all over the country.

But there was one visitor to the shop who they were unable to fit. It was a Saturday afternoon, and Edna and Elsie were standing behind a large glass display counter when, with a sudden crash, the glass-fronted main door burst open. Somewhat startled, they looked up, and there before them, framed in the doorway, stood a bullock peering at them. They prided themselves on providing caps to fit any head, but they felt this to be one challenge they could not accept, so they stood transfixed behind the counter.

The animal came into the shop and then, for reasons known only to itself, decided to reconnoitre upstairs. Sauntering past a glass showcase and a large mirror in the hall, it clattered up the winding, well-polished, lino-covered stairway, passing a stained glass window half-way up. The only person on the upper floor at the time was the cleaning lady, carrying out her duties in the workroom, and a sudden piercing scream announced to Edna and Elsie that the bullock had arrived.

Fortunately, the drover put in an appearance at this point and, with his stick, manoeuvred the bullock back down the stairs. Then, however, the animal turned into a narrow hallway leading to the

The unwelcome "customer".

back entrance, where it came face to face with itself in another mirror. Eventually, much to the ladies' relief, it left via the front door, and the only damage, as Edna delicately put it, was "some rather unpleasant mess on the stairs".

The final closure of H. Rumsey Wells Ltd. left just one mystery which, for years, has puzzled so many people: Why was the Doggie Cap so called? Who better to answer this question than Edna Watling? She was a trifle cautious in her reply.

"Well," she said, "I think it came from the small dog which appeared on the trade mark of the 'Talbot', a popular Rumsey Wells cap of the twenties".

Another of life's mysteries solved!

CHAPTER 10

Green's On The Haymarket.

To say that Norwich has seen many changes since the thirties is, I suppose, to state the obvious, but the face which the city now presents is a very different one from that which I knew so well in my boyhood. Norwich is, indeed, a very different city, with a face that reflects the society it now serves.

One of the most noticeable of all the changes is in the shopping areas, where one cannot help feeling a tinge of regret that there are now so few of the old family concerns. What we now have are, for the most part, branches of large chain stores – the same stores that are to be found in almost every town and city in the kingdom. Somehow, there is not the local feel about them. They have an air of remoteness, with their head offices far away in distant places rather than in the city of which they are a part.

We felt at home with the local businesses. We shared a mutual sense of belonging, and the old family names gave the place a certain sense of identity. There was Chamberlin's overlooking the Market Place, and Willmott's on Prince of Wales Road; Trevor, Page & Co. for furniture, and Louis Marchesi at Langfords for cakes and confectionery; and there was that wonderful trio of drapers, Bunting's, Curl's and Garland's. The list is almost endless, and the great thing about them is that many of the men who gave their names to those firms put a lot back into the city in recompense for what they were taking out. Nowhere was this more marked than in the case of George Green, who established a small chain of outfitter's shops, with his flagship on the Haymarket.

George Green was not a Norfolk man by birth, having been born into a non-conformist family at Cottenham, in Cambridgeshire, on April 24th, 1847. While still a small boy, however, the family moved to Great Yarmouth, where his father, a Baptist minister, became pastor of a chapel in Row 15. Later his father became minister of the chapel in Wellesley Road, and young George was apprenticed to a grocer. This proved not to be much to his liking although, in later years, he readily admitted that the foundations for such business skills as he had acquired were laid over a grocer's counter.

In 1869, at the age of 22, he came to Norwich and opened a hatter's and outfitter's shop at numbers 30 and 32 Rampant Horse Street, living first above the shop and later in Theatre Street. During the course of his lifetime he was destined to live in thirteen different houses, and it is interesting to note that, each time he moved, he went a little bit more upmarket – a sure sign that his business was flourishing.

The Rampant Horse Street business prospered, and he then opened other shops in Red Lion Street, St. Benedict's and Magdalen Street. The latter, however, failed to survive the coming of the trams, for customers who normally shopped there found it convenient to take a ride into the city centre to do their purchasing. Then, at the beginning of this century, he opened his finest shop – the one by which he is best remembered – on the Haymarket.

Green's shop on the Haymarket was very much a symbol of its time, the age when business transactions were carried out in a more leisurely manner and with a bit of style. It was built and furnished in such a way that it was a pleasure to go in. Furthermore, the staff always gave the impression that the customer was doing them a great favour by shopping there – nothing was too much trouble – and this feeling was reflected in the attitude of their customers. People who shopped there felt a degree of pride that they were wearing clothing that came from Green's.

The shop was spacious and rather grand. The walls were covered with lovingly-tended wooden panelling, and on the floor there was a thick Persian-style carpet in a mixture of red and fawn. In those days there was not the present-day concern among businessmen that the floor-space should produce so many pounds per square foot. Hence, there was plenty of room to move around, in spite of the wide variety of features which the shop contained. There were large, attractive showcases and counters, expansive mirrors, and a host of potted palms dotted about all over the place.

There were, of course, chairs at each counter – every shop had them in those days so that the female customers could be seated while their needs were being attended to. Then, in the middle, facing the door there was the cash desk. Shopping in those days was an unhurried occupation. It was not a question of grabbing a garment from a rack and then making one's way, plastic card in

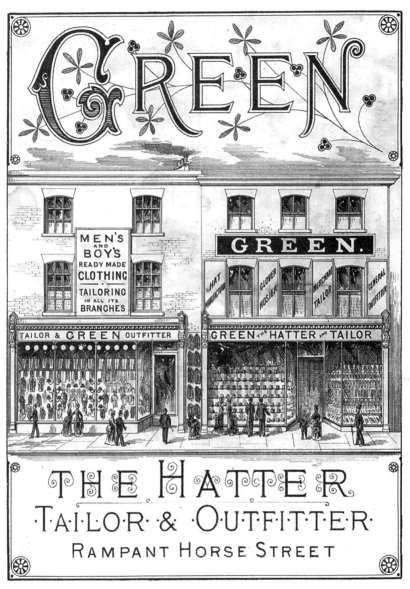

Publicity for George Green's shop at
30 & 32 Rampant Horse Street, Norwich, c.1890.

Next Page: Men's and boys' fashions from Green's,
portrayed before the pagoda in Chapelfield Gardens, late 19th Century.

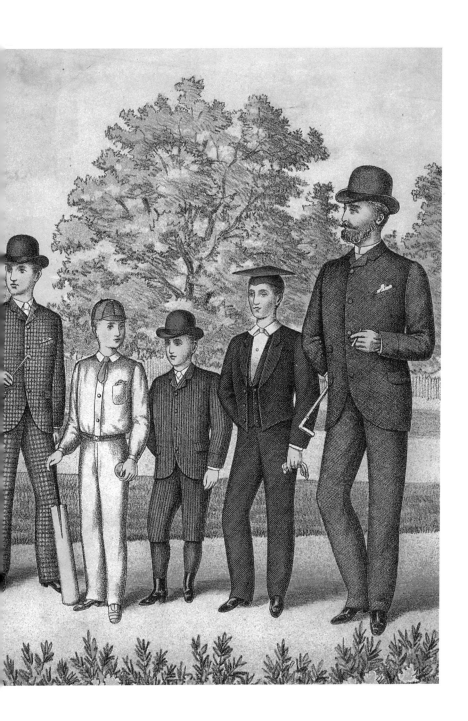

hand, to the nearest check-out. Nothing of the sort! A selection of items was produced from cupboards and drawers and offered to the customer for selection. Then, the choice having been made, a bill was made out for presentation at the cash desk. The cash was received, change given and a written receipt handed over. The selected item was carefully wrapped and, all the while, there was time for conversation. People seemed to talk more in those days!

Much attention was paid to the interests of children, for they were the customers of the future. At one time – I think it must have been before the Great War – there was a large showcase containing a group of stuffed King Charles Spaniels. Few people now remember it, and I have yet to discover its significance.

But there was much more. At the end of the Ready-made department there was a wooden swing with two chair-type seats on which children could swing themselves sick. In another area there was a wooden switchback with two trolleys on which young people could ride. It was a great attraction to children, but something of a distraction to the staff when the air became filled with the ear-piercing shrieks of youngsters pretending to be express trains. Then, of course, there was the famous rocking horse, which must have been there from the very beginning. Countless thousands of youngsters, now having reached a state of maturity, have fond memories of the many imaginary miles they covered on that worthy wooden steed. Every so often it would mysteriously disappear from the shop for a while because, after a period of rough treatment from its young riders, it gave the impression of suffering from an acute attack of mange, and it was taken away to have a new mane and tail fitted. The horse was still there when the shop finally closed in 1960 and then, rumour has it, it went to All Saints' Green to give pleasure to the young customers of Bond's.

On one side of the shop there was a staircase leading up to a balcony and the stock rooms. George Green's office was up there, and he found the balcony a useful observation point from which to keep an eye on the activities of his staff below. From the windows of the stock rooms one looked out onto Hay Hill where, at that time, Sir Thomas Browne sat, head in hand, on the grass between the trees. Now, of course, he has been pushed into a corner and surveys little more than a sea of concrete.

One thing for which Green's was renowned was the excellence of the window displays. On one occasion the display in the Men's

Probably the last picture of Green's shop on the Haymarket, Norwich, not long before it was demolished in 1960.

Clothing window included a large number of live rabbits which drew the attention of passers-by. George Green's grand-daughter Pat, a youngster at the time, remembers it well. "To me," she said, "there seemed to be hundreds". They were in the window to advertise the shop's range of fur gloves, which were then very popular and were, of course, made of rabbit's fur. One cannot help wondering whether the number of rabbits had increased by the time the window was emptied ready for the next display.

On another occasion they had a motor car in the window, but this was by accident rather than by design. A motorist had parked his car on the steep slope of Hay Hill, outside the Haymarket Picture House and facing towards Green's. Off he went and, while he was away, the brakes failed. All of a sudden, right through the store, customers and staff heard a terrific crash and, rushing through to see what had occurred, they found the car with its bonnet proudly on display, surrounded by fragments of broken glass. It caused quite a bit of excitement but puzzled the owner of the car who, on his return, wondered why it was not where he had left it!

There was one aspect of Green's which has always slightly puzzled me. They had two delivery vans, one large and one small, both dark mauve in colour and with the inscription "Green's (Nch) Ltd." inscribed on the side in flowing copper plate writing. These vehicles were manned by a driver and a junior, similarly attired in mauve trench coats and mauve peaked caps. But, I ask myself, why mauve? The firm's delivery labels and billheads were printed in green, so why not the vans? Just another of life's little mysteries.

George Green's staff were numerous and, for the most part, very loyal, many spending their entire working lives in the service of the Company.

The General Manager was Mr. Shelbourn, who suffered mental anguish at seeing his staff engaged in idle conversation, even when there were no customers awaiting attention. They should at least, he thought, give the impression of being busy – "Sparkle! Sparkle!" he would cry.

Maudie Allman was the office supremo for almost a lifetime, while few people could remember seeing Miss Wright, the head of Juveniles, clothed other than in a dress of velvety chenille.

Frank Mills was a legend with a tremendous line in patter, and it was claimed that he could sell anything to anybody. There was,

George Green during his year of office as Lord Mayor, 1919-20.

however, one occasion when his enthusiasm got the better of him. A lady in the process of buying a travelling trunk asked for an assurance that it was strong.

"Strong?" he said. "Just watch this," and he proceeded to jump on it. Sadly, his feet went clean through.

The firm's Beau Brummel was the bow-tied Mr. Hannant, never without a rolled umbrella whatever the weather. Harold Rose of Ready-mades was another dapper little man, but the most inspired appointment must surely have been that, as window dresser, of Mr. Bailey, who just about topped five feet in his socks.

Those, and many more, were the folk on whom George Green kept an eye from his vantage point up on the balcony. Yet, active though he was in the business life of the city, he still found time to immerse himself deeply in civic and religious matters. He was an Alderman on the City Council and, in 1919, he became Lord Mayor. He was also a River Commissioner, a post for which he was well qualified. He had a great liking for the open air life and especially sailing, a pursuit in which he encouraged his sons to take an active part. He had a succession of sailing craft and was highly regarded in boating circles.

Religious matters also received his full attention, and he played a prominent part in founding the Baptist Church at Cromer. He was President of Norfolk Baptist Association and Chairman of the East Anglian Federation of Free Churches. He also held various offices in the Y.M.C.A. and, not surprisingly, he was also a magistrate. Thus, it can be truly said that he was putting a lot back into the city from which he derived his income.

Eventually he moved to number 378 Unthank Road, which many people will know better as that splendid pile, Eaton Grange. Later he was off again, this time to Pakefield, where his near neighbour was Benjamin Britten. Then, on becoming Lord Mayor, he returned to Norwich and took up residence in an extremely splendid house set in very spacious grounds in the shadow of the Roman Catholic Cathedral. This was The Plantation, the garden of which has, in recent years, been "rediscovered" by a group of enthusiasts who are endeavouring to restore it to its former grandeur. Incidentally, the original owner of The Plantation was Henry Trevor, one of the partners in Trevor, Page & Co. During George Green's year as Lord Mayor, the Plantation Garden was the scene of many fetes and civic occasions, and he remained in residence there until his death on January 3rd, 1928, at the age

George and Emma Green in their garden at The Plantation, 1920.

of 80. From there, they took him to that most appropriate of final resting places, The Rosary, where he joined so many of the men and women who had helped to mould the future of their native city.

It was the end of an era but, though the worthy George Green had left the scene, the business continued to prosper under the leadership of his son, Tim. Gradually, however, the face of the city was changing, as was also the lifestyle of its citizens. Eventually, in 1960, Green's reached the end of its life. There was a bittersweet party for the staff, followed by a sale of the contents of the shop. Arthur Chapman, the Norwich butcher, bought the wooden panelling to beautify his home in Mile End Road; the rocking horse found pastures new at Bond's.

Then, in came the bulldozers to clear the site to make room for a modern superstore. Down came the old shop, together with the Livingstone Hotel, in which Green's had provided facilities for commercial travellers to store and display their wares. But, perhaps saddest of all, down also came the old Elizabethan building which many people believe to have been the Garden House of Sir Thomas Browne. The authorities compromised by affixing to a wall in Orford Place a plaque indicating that Sir Thomas "lived near here".

But the memory of that rather splendid outfitter's shop still lingers, as does that of the man who founded it so many years ago. Of all the descriptions of the man which I have heard, I like best the one given to me by his grand-daughter, remembering him when she was a small child.

"Grandpa terrified me to death," she said. "There was I, a tiny thing with Mummy holding my hand and Grandpa looking down at me: 'Well, young lady, and how are you today?' He seemed enormous – it was like looking up at a skyscraper, with my neck extended backwards and my eyes travelling upwards over a pear-shaped abdomen graced with a gold watch chain and seeing a pair of steel blue eyes looking down at me over a white Imperial beard surmounted by a white moustache. He wore boots which were fastened at the sides with little black spherical buttons which always fascinated me as they reminded me of blackcurrants. No doubt he was fond of me in his peculiar way. Like all the Greens, his bark was worse than his bite".

CHAPTER 11

Sir George White.

"Everybody who came seemed
to be under a sense of personal loss".

Thus spoke one of thousands who congregated at the Rosary Cemetery in Norwich to pay their last respects at the funeral of Sir George White M.P. The year was 1912, and never before could any man have earned such an overwhelming show of respect, admiration and, indeed, sheer personal love as was afforded to that distinguished son of Norwich.

If one wished to be pernickety, one could question the title of "son of Norwich", for he was not born in the city, but some ninety miles away in the small Lincolnshire town of Bourne. Such a fact, however, pales into insignificance when set against the achievements of his seventy-two years – achievements which brought such lasting benefit, not only to his adopted city, but to the country in general. As a shoe manufacturer and merchant, it has been rightly said that he did more than any single man of his time to build up the national prestige of Norwich in relation to its staple industry. Yet this was only one facet of the man, for he was so many-sided in his interests and influences, and he had such sharpness of mind and firmness of character that, wherever he came in contact with the life of his time, he left a lasting impact.

Looking back over the life of George White, one gets the distinct impression that much of it was influenced by the hand of Fate. Indeed, it seems that Dame Fortune was already making her arrangements in his years of infancy, for it was in 1842, when little George was just two years old, that a certain Robert Tillyard started a leather currying business in Elm Hill in Norwich. There, with the tanning and preparing of leather for bootmakers and saddlers, business flourished to such an extent that bigger premises were soon needed. To Robert Tillyard, however, this presented a problem, for he had insufficient capital to finance such a move. Then it was that Fate played its hand – in the unlikely form of one James Warnes Howlett of Sedgeford Hall in West Norfolk. He had no wish to be other than a sleeping partner, but he had what was then the considerable sum of ten thousand pounds which he was prepared to invest in the business. Thus the move was made to premises in Princes Street, followed a few years later by a further removal to still larger premises in Swan Lane.

At this point, James Warnes Howlett began to play a more active part, largely on the financial side of things, and, being aware of the probability of continuing growth, tried to persuade his son, John Godfery Howlett, to enter the business. This young man, however, being of a retiring disposition, was somewhat apprehensive of city life and the world of commerce, a feeling not uncommon in those days among those who had been brought up in the country amidst agricultural pursuits. His father's vision of the future, however, was soon to become a reality.

His son joined the Company, which then became known as Tillyard & Howlett, and then, in 1856, the business was removed to the site on St. George's Plain which, steadily expanding, was to be its home for the rest of its existence. There, in the fullness of time, the self-confessed 'clod-hopping farmer's son' was destined to become senior partner of a business with the biggest shoe factory under one roof in the British Isles. Yet, through all the years of success, nothing changed him in his contact with the people around him. The memories most frequently recalled by those who knew him in those later years were his 'old-world courtesy and generous temper'.

John Godfery Howlett started his career at the bottom of the ladder. It must be remembered that the manufacture of boots and shoes was still a thing of the future. Tillyard & Howlett were simply curers and suppliers of leather to all who required it, and it was this to which he applied himself. For a time, his main occupation was the cutting out of leather for fishermen's thigh-boots, though he also sold parcels of leather to shoe repairers and bespoke shoemakers, as well as to harness-makers and saddlers. Then, within two years, he had so gained the confidence of his father and the Tillyards that they put him 'on the road' as a commercial traveller. For ever after that time it was the practice to put the sons of the partners on the road for a period of experience in the selling of the products of the Company, and it was on one of John Godfery Howlett's trips that Dame Fortune played her second card.

His last call of the week was at a shop at Bourne in Lincolnshire, and it was there that he was to meet his future partner. The shop was run by Thomas and Mary White, who were highly respected customers of the firm of Tillyard & Howlett, buying considerable quantities of leather from them. John Godfery Howlett, then aged 24, was greatly impressed by the cheerful nature and readiness to help shown by their son George, nearly ten years his junior. The boy's interest in the various matters of business discussed between his father and the traveller from Norwich also did not go unnoticed, and Howlett had already formed a good opinion of young George when Thomas White asked for help concerning his son's future life.

"We want him to get on in the world, and he's too good for our small business," he said. "We've been wondering whether you could find him a place at Norwich".

Rather fortuitously, it was the time when the firm had just moved to St. George's Plain and was undergoing great expansion. On his return to Norwich, John Godfery spoke to his father and the Tillyards about the boy, praising his apparent ability in most enthusiastic terms. As a result, in 1856, sixteen-year-old George White joined the business as a junior clerk.

One of his first actions on arriving in Norwich was to join St. Mary's Baptist Church down by the factory, thus beginning an association which was to continue for the rest of his life.

He had a great yearning for knowledge and eagerly sought out the educational facilities which Norwich offered. They were, of course, very limited in those days but, even so, the city must have seemed like a veritable haven of learning compared with Bourne. He even attended classes with solicitor John Withers Dowson, who offered instruction to anybody keen enough to rise sufficiently early. Before starting his work at the factory at 8 o'clock in the morning, he would go to Mr. Dowson's offices and have free lessons in mathematics and other subjects, along with other eager youngsters of his generation.

After a year or two, in accordance with tradition, George White went on the road in search of orders for Tillyard & Howlett's products. It was a task into which he threw himself with great dedication, but one which would have sorely tested a man with less strength of character, for he was a teetotaller in a world of hard-drinking commercial travellers. Not only did he steadfastly refuse to buy alcoholic drinks for the others – he also declined their offers of similar refreshment. He was not popular in that particular branch of society.

During the course of the years that followed, George White served in practically every capacity in the business, eventually reaching the position of general manager. Then, in 1876, he became co-partner with John Godfery Howlett, the man who had recommended him for employment with the Company exactly twenty years previously. Even more significantly, the name of the Company became Howlett & White – the title which was to bring the Company such glory in the years ahead.

There can be no doubt that the two men, so alike in many ways yet differing in others, made a splendid combination. The 'old-world courtesy and generous temper' of the one and the austere nature and sense of justice of the other blended together to form an ideal partnership. Making money was never the be-all and end-all of their existence. It was, perhaps, the main driving force but, as far as circumstances allowed, the moral and religious dictates of their consciences had a strict bearing on their conduct in business – and in life in general.

By this time, John Godfery's father had retired and later died, leaving the two younger men to set out on the great adventure of building up the business. Both were now married and with young families, their wives being sisters, and both were deacons of St. Mary's Baptist Chapel in Duke Street. Whenever possible, it was the custom for the two men to attend early morning service at St. Mary's before starting their day's work.

They immediately began an ambitious building programme on St. George's Plain, in the process of which many old buildings were swept away. Down came a grocer's shop, a barber's, a pawnbroker's and the 'Shakespeare' public house. Down, also, came the attractive residence of Dr. Addison, father of Amelia, who later married the celebrated portrait painter, Sir John Opie.

In the rebuilding that followed, the senior partner was happy to leave the development of the boot and shoe manufacturing side in the hands of his younger colleague. This was a challenge that George White gladly accepted and, in doing so, he brought the firm of Howlett & White (later the Norvic Shoe Company) to a position of national prominence in the industry. At the same time, however, his self-appointed role as a reformer and social worker demanded that he should at all times be conscious of his duties to his fellow men.

In some ways it could be said that George White was the very epitome of Victorian ambition, rising, as he did, from somewhat humble beginnings to achieve wealth, political power and public recognition. His craving for success, however, was not that of a man seeking the pinnacles of power from which to look down upon his fellow men. Just the reverse – he wanted to take them up there with him. As an employer, he made it plain that every member of his workforce, even those engaged in the most menial of duties, should have the right to equal support in the affairs of the Howlett & White 'family'. Nor did it stop there, for he preached the same message to his fellow industrialists.

"Many of us," he said, "are employers, and our relationship with those in our employ should be fair and equal. As citizens we should strive to have the best things common to all. This is not a question of dividing money or property, but of equality of opportunity, of destroying privilege, and placing within reach of the people the advantage of moderate leisure, recreation, education, social advancement and the best of spiritual influences".

Those words constituted part of a speech which he made in 1904, and he went on to speak in an equally forthright manner on the subjects of education, the housing situation, temperance, freedom and religious tolerance – all of them matters which provided the driving force to his life. There can be little doubt that George White was endowed with tremendous energy, as well as an outstanding ability to turn from one subject to another with consummate ease and with barely a second's hesitation.

He was a member of the Reform Club and of the National Liberal Club; in his younger days he enjoyed a game of cricket, and later in life it was golf. But it is significant that he regarded these merely as brief diversions – his chief relaxation was work. I suppose this could be said of many men of note, but there can be few of whom it was more true.

Even the briefest of glances at George White's Lincolnshire boyhood gives a clear indication that he was destined for a political career. There, at Bourne, he recalled running up the Liberal colours during the election of 1852. He was a mere twelve years of age, but he avidly read all the political news of the day and could recite the constituencies of every Member of Parliament. Three years after his arrival in Norwich, still barely twenty years old, he became the honorary secretary of the Liberal Association in the city. Then, in 1876, he was elected to Norwich Council, and in due course he became an Alderman and Sheriff of the City.

He was chairman of the Norwich School Board for fifteen years

The Shakespeare Tavern and the house of Amelia Opie's father, both demolished to make way for Howlett & White's shoe factory.

Looking after the workers. Inauguration of the Norvic Pension Fund, St. Andrew's Hall, Norwich, 1920.

and, when it was superseded by the Education Committee, he became chairman of that also. I think it can truly be said that, apart from his work in the cause of religion, education was the prime interest in his life. Hence, it is not difficult to appreciate the great feeling of satisfaction he must have experienced when, in their last act before handing over to the Education Committee, the School Board unanimously decided that one of the new schools they were building should be called the George White School.

"What more appropriate tribute," asked a writer of the day, "what grander memorial could any man ask for than that those bricks and stones should be built to perpetuate the name of one who, many years ago, made the education of the children of the working classes possible, and even popular?"

The next, and seemingly inevitable, step in George White's career came in 1900, when he was elected to Parliament as the Member for North-West Norfolk in succession to Joseph Arch. He gained a majority of just 476 over Sir William Ffolkes, but it was a major triumph considering the popularity of Sir William in that part of the county. At the General Election of 1906 he increased his majority to 2,800, and he comfortably held the seat in the two elections which took place in 1910.

During his career in the House of Commons, one can do no more than speculate upon the nature of the relationship between George White, with his strong views on temperance, and his near neighbour in the House, the Member for Norwich – none other than one of the city's biggest brewers, Sir Harry Bullard.

Prior to his election as Sheriff in 1888, George White and his family had been living in a pleasantly-situated house near the beginning of Unthank Road, just a few steps away from Trinity United Reform Church. Their back garden, in fact, ran through to Henry Trevor's Plantation Garden high up by the edge of a former chalk pit. Remembering his Lincolnshire boyhood, he named the house Bourne Villa – later it was to become the Fairway Hotel, and now a branch of the City's social services. It was around the time of his year of office as Sheriff that the steadily increasing size of his family (the final tally of which was one son and seven daughters) made a move to larger accommodation necessary. Hence, the Whites transferred to The Grange, almost at the county end of Unthank Road. At that time, the extensive grounds stretched down to Unthank Road, but more recently-built houses now screen the house from view.

George White at the height of his career.

Not only was The Grange more suited to the needs of a large family, but it was also more in keeping with George White's status when, in 1907, he received his knighthood. The people of the city were delighted, for they were proud of their adopted son. Then, in 1910, he was made an Honorary Freeman of the City of Norwich, his name joining those of illustrious predecessors who included Wellington, Nelson, Pitt and Peel.

By then his life had only a limited time to run and, on May 11th, 1912, he drew his last breath. Even then, however, he maintained the strength of spirit which had seen him through life. He knew his end was near and, growing steadily weaker, he spent most of his time in peaceful sleep. Then, without warning and in spite of his extreme weakness, he suddenly opened his eyes and cried out in a firm voice, "What are we waiting for?"

The funeral, in the words of the Press reporter, was "one of the most extraordinary manifestations of sympathy and public interest ever witnessed in Norwich. The windows of shops and private houses far beyond the line of the route covered by the procession were shaded". It is said that, as a mark of respect for the man who had spent a lifetime preaching about the perils of drink, most of the city's public houses were closed. The Reverend J.H. Shakespeare preached the memorial sermon at St. Mary's Baptist Church and then, as the cortège made its slow progress along Tombland and down Prince of Wales Road, groups of people, heads bowed, stood in silent tribute to the city's adopted son.

At least three thousand people gathered at the Rosary and, as the time of the interment approached, the crowd grew larger with the addition of prominent citizens of all shades of political and religious opinion. Standing with the deacons and elders of the Free Churches were the head of the Roman Catholic community, representatives of the Established Church, and the renowned Non-conformist leader, Dr. John Clifford, who offered up prayers at the graveside.

Much reference was made to his "untiring industry, clearly-seen purpose, resolution and shrewd judgement". Yet, perhaps the best epitaph lies in the two simple lines once quoted by George White in one of his speeches:

If each before his own door swept,
Then all the streets were clean.

CHAPTER 12
George Reeve – Printer.

To those of us who enjoy playing with words, I suppose the introduction of the printing press must rank as one of man's greatest innovations. The spoken word is a transient thing; without the aid of memory it can fade away as quickly as it is uttered. But the printed word has a degree of permanence that can enable it to last for centuries.

In Norfolk it is interesting to note how branches of the printing industry sprang up and steadily became part of the traditional face of certain places. Norwich, of course, is a prime example, especially since John Jarrold brought his business from Woodbridge and established it in the city in 1832, but the same is true of several of our market towns. Fakenham, for example, long carried on that tradition whilst, in North Walsham and Holt, Rounce and Wortley have had their presses rolling throughout living memory. Then there is Aylsham, where Barnwell's have already notched up a century and a half.

In Wymondham, the second half of the nineteenth century saw a veritable clutch of such people, with the Forster family being particularly prominent and a certain Mr. Dightam publishing a local paper, *The Wymondham Advertiser,* from his grandly-named Minerva Printing Works. The most successful printer of that era, however, was Henry Girling Stone who, in 1886, established his business on Town Green. There it flourished for over a hundred years until its sudden demise in 1992.

Shortly after the end of the First World War, Henry Girling Stone took on as an apprentice a young man who had returned from service in the trenches and wanted to make printing his career. They were the days when untrained youngsters could not expect to start work for anything approaching a living wage – they had first to "learn a trade". The length of an apprenticeship at that time was seven years, and the young man who thus bound his future to Stone's was George Raymond Reeve.

George duly completed his apprenticeship and before long, being a man of ambition, he became fired with the idea of starting his own business. This he did in 1928, offering his services within a few hundred yards of Stone's premises. He rented a small room behind what was at that time Walter Lane's gents' outfitters shop. The fact that it was a small room was of little concern to him, for the only equipment he had at that time was one case of type, a very small printing machine and a carving knife for cutting up the paper.

To be completely truthful, he had one other thing – a loan of £175 from the British Legion, which he contracted to pay back in annual instalments over a number of years.

All his life George was a man ambitious to succeed, not for purely monetary gain but because of the sense of achievement it gave him. Consequently, it is not surprising that his business flourished, and he eventually moved to larger premises – he could hardly have moved to smaller ones – opposite St. Becket's Chapel in Church Street. Then he got the urge to expand further and, just along the street, on Damgate Corner, he opened up a retail stationery business. Nor was this the end of his expanding empire, for soon he was to acquire what, to my mind, is one of the loveliest shops in Wymondham, and it became the Old Beams Bookshop in Market Street. At this time fortune smiled upon him, for the educational establishment which is now Wymondham College was then a Teachers' Training College, and the students bought their course books from him.

Meanwhile, other things were going on in George Reeve's life. One of the best-known and most highly-regarded families in the business life of the town at that time was that of the Standleys, in which there were one son, Eric, and three daughters, all of whom duly married. Elsie married a Methodist minister and moved away from the area, but the others stayed close to their roots. Marie married Reg Seager from Norwich, who managed one of the Standley shops, while Doris chose George Reeve as her life partner. In the years that followed, Doris and George were not blessed with children, but Marie and Reg had a son, Brian. Then, in 1950, Brian Seager, having completed his apprenticeship (by then only two years) with Jarrolds in Norwich, joined his Uncle George in the printing business.

In 1960 George Reeve turned his empire into a limited company, and then, in 1971, there came another move. Ever since 1881, on the corner of Damgate Street and Market Street, there had stood the grocery and drapery store founded by Edward 'Ginger' Clarke

George Reeve (right) in a happy family moment.

and later carried on by his son and daughter, Harry and Emma. That shop and its proprietor were legendary and merit a book all to themselves. It dated from the days when some of the staff "lived in", and Harry was a delightful throwback to another age – a perfect double for Mr. Pickwick. But in 1969 Harry died and later, when the business closed, Geo. R. Reeve Ltd. moved in.

The business prospered in its new home, but then, in 1977, George Reeve died, leaving his nephew to take the helm.

George Reeve had been a lifelong devout Methodist, to whom his Faith was everything. He always said that it was his Faith that had carried him through the mud-filled trenches of Flanders. He was a prominent local preacher, much-loved all round the Circuit, and secretary of the local Preachers' Mutual Aid Association.

One person who cherishes fond memories of the man is Gwen Cooper of Hempnall, who was brought up within the fellowship of the local Methodist Church, where her father, Jack Stammers, was organist for over sixty years. She recalls George as being one of the four 'greats', the others being Gerald Stammers (her great-uncle), Lewis Blackburn of Pulham Market and that other fine man of Wymondham, Wesley Corston.

"I remember so well," she said, "this serious but kindly man with the twinkling eyes and his thoughtful sermons, delivered over the heads of the congregation into the middle distance. He would come down from the pulpit after the Benediction to make sure he shook hands with everybody who was there, and he was always most appreciative of the singing and my father's music at the organ".

Music was, indeed, George's other love. He had a fine voice, much in demand with the Amateur Operatics at the Old Town Hall in Wymondham. In chapel he delighted in taking care of the descants, and he never needed much persuasion to sing a solo.

As a business man he was always very straight and to the point – sometimes, indeed, to the point of bluntness. There were occasionally some people who misunderstood his bluntness but, as one of his former customers put it, "You knew where you stood with George, even when he appeared stern. He had a sparkle in his eyes, and even when he was being serious his eyes kept on smiling – you couldn't help feeling that he was your friend".

By way of a postscript to the business life of George Raymond Reeve, I recently had the chance of studying his first balance sheet. It covered a period of 17 months from November 8th, 1928 to March 31st, 1930, and the salient items read as follows:

Gross Turnover: £579 0s 1d.

Wages: £49 6s 3d.

Repaid British Legion: £23 10s 0d.

NET PROFIT: £12 6s 2d. (for 17 months!)

One day, as we sipped coffee, I asked Brian whether he thought George always intended that he should eventually take over. A little smile crossed his face and he said:

"One day, when I was about ten years old, Uncle George gave me a Charles Dickens book. It was 'Great Expectations' – I think that's what he had".

It is, perhaps, strange for a writer to be writing about his publisher, but Brian Seager is friend first and publisher second. Hence I find it easy to express my belief that, if George was able to return and see what his nephew has made of his Company, he would be more than a little pleased that his expectations had been so well fulfilled.

He would also feel a touch of poignancy, for in 1994 Geo. R. Reeve Ltd. left the retail shop to function on Damgate Corner and transferred the printing business to the former premises of H.G. Stone & Co. where, all those years ago, George served his apprenticeship. The wheel has come full circle!

4

A Posy of People

Some men are born for great things,
Some are born for small:
Some — it is not recorded
Why they were born at all.

Augustus Jessopp,
Rector of Scarning, 1891.

CHAPTER 13

Tom Thackeray and Guide Anna.

Captain Thackeray was a man who lived life to the full. Indeed, his life was far removed from that mapped out for him when he made his entry into the world at Norton Subcourse in 1884. His father, the Reverend A.T.J. Thackeray, was Vicar of that parish for no less than forty years from 1885 onwards and was, furthermore, a great benefactor of his own church. In 1893 he presented two bells to hang in the tower with the existing four, and in 1898, when the church was reseated in oak, he shared the cost with Nicholas Henry Bacon of Raveningham Hall. But any hopes he might have had that his son would follow in his footsteps were soon to be dashed.

Young Master Thackeray, who could claim kinship with the author of *Vanity Fair,* was christened Thomas Frederick Makepeace, and it soon became apparent that he had no great leanings towards the Church. At a very early age he developed an affinity with horses which was to dominate his later life and, by the time he was ten years old, he was regularly riding to hounds. During the First World War he served in East Africa in the King's African Rifles and then, when hostilities ceased, he settled in Wymondham to start a career in farming.

In 1920 he was appointed Huntsman of the Norwich Staghounds, a post which was to take precedence over everything else in his life, and he lost little time in giving up the farm and moving into lodgings at 'The Rookery' in Vicar Street.

His landlady in that splendid house, where he was to remain for the rest of his life, was Miss Anna Martha Smith, unquestionably one of the most well-loved residents of Wymondham at that time. Known to all simply as 'Guide Anna' because of her position as Captain of the local Girl Guides detachment, she was a lady of great kindness, with a big smile and a sympathetic word for everybody. Much of her life centred around the nearby Abbey Church, where she was a Sunday School teacher and a regular attender at services. Evensong was her favourite, and her neighbours always knew what the last hymn had been, for she would sing it again with great gusto as she walked the few hundred yards to her home at the end of the service.

Guide Anna's principal source of income was the small school which she ran in her spacious rooms. It was a fairly modest establishment – usually not more than thirty or so children – but it had a great reputation as a centre of happiness. Even today there are people who, not having been privileged to attend that little haven of learning, recall the feeling of envy with which they regarded the fortunate few who did.

As a second string to her bow, Guide Anna had two gentlemen lodgers, one of whom was habitually the Abbey curate. The other, for something like thirty years, was Captain Thackeray, and what an unlikely pair they made! There was Anna, the lover of children, a model of sobriety and pillar of the Church; and there was whisky-drinking Tom, living life in top gear and never getting nearer to the Abbey than the Green Dragon, just round the corner. But Anna forgave him his trespasses and tolerated his whims, even to the extent of habitually laying out his entire accumulation of table silver before he would sit down to his solitary meal.

There is no doubt that Tom was very well-liked, though some of the younger generation tended to be wary of him because of their belief that he was of uncertain temper if he had not taken a few drinks. It has been said that, in spite of his third Christian name, one thing he was certainly not noted for was making peace. Yet I am convinced that there was not a drop of malice in the man.

Tom Thackeray and I had more than one confrontation – always, I must say, on a friendly basis. He knew that my view of some so-called country sports did not tally with his, but we understood each other. I never tried to make him desist from his pursuit of deer (such action would have been futile anyway), but we both knew each other's views and agreed to differ.

There was one occasion when, as I stood by my front gate talking to a neighbour, our conversation was suddenly halted by the appearance of a deer, foaming at the mouth and in obvious distress. It crossed what was then the main A11 trunk road and, lumbering down my neighbour's garden, disappeared in the direction of a copse at Downham Grove. Within minutes, along came Tom, together with the hounds and his whipper-in, George Marshall.

Anna Smith and pupils outside her school in Vicar Street, Wymondham, 1928.

Guide Anna enjoying a meal in camp, 1924.

"Seen a deer come this way?" he asked.

"Yes," I replied.

"Which way did it go?"

"That way," I said, indicating the opposite direction to the one the deer had taken.

Tom turned his horse and took the hounds off on a false trail. But it couldn't last. They had gone little more than fifty yards when the hounds picked up the scent and, wheeling round, took off in the direction of Downham Grove. Tom came along and, pausing as he passed me, he looked down at me and said quietly, "You might fool me, but you can't fool the hounds".

"Perhaps that shows which of you has the greater intelligence," I replied.

It was all rather schoolboyish, but we were both happy. He had made his point and, as for me, well, I had at least assuaged my conscience.

Of course, there was never a 'kill' at the end of the chase, for the deer were the property of the Hunt and spent the greater part of their lives grazing peacefully on an enclosed area of meadow land at Winfarthing. But it was the way in which, every so often, their tranquil, semi-domesticated existence was rudely shattered to meet the demands of the chase that led me to the opinion that the activity was not exactly a sporting one. On the day of the hunt one of the beasts would be selected, loaded into a horse box and carted to the scene of the day's sport. There it would be released and, after a suitable pause, horses and hounds – the latter brought from their kennels at Suton – would set off in pursuit. Hence, great efforts were made to apprehend the quarry, and Tom was once known to wade into the waters of the River Tas to recover a deer that had taken refuge there. The animal that I had seen disappearing into the cover of Downham Grove, however, finally reached the garden of a Cringleford householder who locked it in her shed and refused the Hunt access to it until a ransom was paid as a donation to charity!

Tom Thackeray was not just a dedicated huntsman – he was a fine and fearless horseman, and I had more than a sneaking regard for him. He had a slight deformity of one arm, the result of an explosion when he had been tinkering with an oil engine in his farming days, but he made light of this handicap and most people were unaware of it. He claimed that he had never been unseated by his horse, but this was not strictly true. There was one occasion when Alfred Munnings was out with the Hunt and Tom made the mistake of setting his horse at a fence that the animal considered to be too testing. It stopped dead in its tracks, sending Tom through the air and into the bottom of a ditch. As Tom crawled out, Munnings made a sketch of the scene and gave it to one of the Hunt servants.

When it was a question of horsemanship, Tom was always in control, but the same could not be said of his ability at driving a motor car. His life was liberally sprinkled with mishaps when at the wheel of his Rover 14, most of them, it must be said, occasioned by his addiction to whisky. There was the occasion when, while driving through Wicklewood, he had a collision with a roadside tree. The accident happened, rather conveniently, outside the home of the Rt. Rev. Edwin Frederick Robins, Vicar of the parish and also assistant bishop and honorary canon of Norwich. Tom decided against seeking help from 'The Bishop', however, and, bloody but unbowed, staggered further along the road and down a long farm drive to the home of an acquaintance. He knew where he could find the right kind of medicine!

Tom garaged his car in Underwood's Yard in Middleton Street and, in spite of the numerous occasions on which he carried out this manoeuvre, he never quite mastered it. My friend Ted Fowler recalls the last occasion on which he saw him. It was the afternoon of an autumn day in 1952 and, returning from a Meet, Tom drove down Market Street, and started the sharp turn into Underwood's Yard. Unfortunately, he misjudged the turn and hit the bumper of a parked car. The occupant, who was writing up some notes at the time, looked up in alarm. Tom then backed up and came forward again, but once more he hit the parked car. He was not a man to give up without a struggle but, as he reversed the car in preparation for a third attempt, the occupant of the car jumped out and ran up the street to fetch a policeman. Once again Tom came forward, and yet again he hit the back of the other car. At that point he gave up and just sat there, his head bowed over the steering wheel.

Within minutes the man returned with a policeman and, between them, they assisted Tom out of his car and, supporting him on either side, headed up Market Street towards the Police Station. Tom was still wearing his white breeches, but he had changed out of his riding boots into shoes, revealing his thin bare legs which just wouldn't support him.

Tom's fondness for whisky was, of course, well-known to the

Tom Thackeray leading the Norwich Staghounds away from the Green Dragon, Wymondham, 1936.

local constabulary and, on one occasion when he was apprehended and charged with being drunk in charge of a motor vehicle, a Police van was standing by to transport him to the Station. Tom offered no resistance. He almost fell out of his car, climbed into the van on his hands and knees and promptly fell asleep.

At another time, after enjoying a game of bowls at Winfarthing, he was driving back to Wymondham with his pair of woods lying on the back shelf of the car. His sobriety was not in question at this time but, as so often happened with Tom, he suddenly found it necessary to apply his brakes with maximum force and urgency. The car shuddered to a halt – but the bowls failed to do likewise. They shot forward, one on either side of his head, and crashed through the windscreen.

Tom Thackeray was certainly a larger-than-life character and a man not easily forgotten. There are still people who remember seeing him fall into the fire at Stoke Red Lion when his elbow slipped off the mantelpiece on which he was leaning. Tales of his exploits are legion, but the best of all must concern the occasion, just after the war, when the Hunt found itself on a local airfield, with the hounds heading down the runway in full cry just as a Stirling bomber was taking off. The pilot managed to get the plane off the ground in time to miss them, but the Station Commander, who was in a jeep on the airfield at the time, followed them in hot pursuit, firing a revolver in a frantic effort to stop them. Tragedy was averted, but Tom said afterwards that there was nothing that he could have done about it. Once the hounds were on the scent and in full cry they would have run to their deaths!

Tom Thackeray retired in May 1953 and, ten years later, public pressure brought about the abolition of deer carting. That decision would have saddened old Tom, but he was not there to see it. His hectic life had come to a sudden end in April, 1955, at the age of 71, in the lodgings in Vicar Street where Guide Anna had looked after him to the end. He is said to have left a considerable estate for those days, but there was only a small bequest for Anna. That dear lady, however, was always a great forgiver – she used the money to buy hymn books for the Abbey 'in memory of Captain Thackeray'.

For his funeral service they took him into the Abbey, suitably filled with local gentry and his many sporting contacts. Then, as red-coated huntsmen blew 'Gone Away', the cortège left for burial at his birthplace in Norton Subcourse.

CHAPTER 14

A Truly Gentle Man.

By the time the people of Norwich had ushered in the New Year of 1941 they were well on the way to becoming battle-hardened veterans of World War II. The air raid sirens had already wailed out their mournful message on no fewer than 580 occasions and, although the vast majority of these had brought no hostile action to the city, there were other nights when death and destruction had rained down from the skies. On the nights when no bombs came, there was the tension of lying in bed or huddling in the shelters and listening to the drone of the planes making their way to the west to some more distant target and then, in the early hours of the morning, heading back to their bases across the Channel.

February 18th, 1941 was one such night. The alert had sounded soon after 11 p.m. and the succession of enemy aircraft had made their way across the city. Then there was the lull until, their mission accomplished, they retraced their flight path on the way home and, once again, peace reigned in the skies. But, on that night, there was more to come.

At precisely five minutes past five in the morning, a lone bomber, presumably a straggler from the pack, dropped a single missile on one of the most densely populated areas of the city. There was a tremendous explosion, accompanied by a huge cloud of dust, as the bomb – or was it a parachute mine? – scored a direct hit on the Vauxhall Tavern, totally destroying that hostelry. All around it there was a vast area of devastation, far greater than anything yet seen in Norwich. Sixteen houses in Vauxhall Street were demolished, and the blast had spread through to Horace Street, Walpole Street and Coach & Horses Street, where some three dozen homes had been similarly devastated. Many other houses were too dangerous to enter and, by that single bomb, no less than 140 people had been rendered homeless.

Police and rescue workers were quickly on the scene, and they, horrified by the sight that greeted them, stared in disbelief at the extent of the devastation. Then, aided by a vast army of volunteers, they set to work, tearing at the rubble with bare hands to release the victims – some mercifully unhurt, some injured, and others already beyond any help they could give.

It was while this work was going on that an almost unbelievable sight was seen. From the rubble of one of the most severely damaged houses in Vauxhall Street, where it was thought that nobody could possibly have survived, there suddenly emerged three figures – a man and two women. They were Eddie Codling, his wife Flo and their daughter Dinky – and Dinky was carrying a budgie in a cage! On the outbreak of war, Eddie had rigged up an electricity supply in the cellar of the house and converted it into sleeping quarters. That was where they had spent every night – and the budgie always went down there with them.

When, on that February night, their house came tumbling down around them, there was no panic – Eddie was not that kind of man. Having ensured that they had all come through the experience unscathed, the important thing was to make themselves as presentable as possible for the climb up through the rubble and into public view. For Flo and Dinky that problem was readily solved simply by donning coats over their night attire. Eddie, however, was always punctilious about propriety, and he had rather more difficulty in finding suitable clothing to wear over his pyjamas. By the time he eventually led his little family into the gaze of the many onlookers, he had donned a pair of policeman's trousers – he was a special constable – and an overcoat which had been his mother-in-law's; what made it all the more embarrassing was the fact that he had to remain garbed in that fashion for some 24 hours before something more suitable was found.

It is a matter of some regret to me that, in those years of war, I knew nothing of Eddie Codling's existence. Indeed, many more years were to pass before our first meeting. By then, having lost both his wife and his daughter, he was living alone in a cosy flat on the southern fringe of Norwich and steadily approaching his ninetieth birthday. He was an avid listener to Radio Norfolk and, having heard me speak of something which interested him, he wrote to me with his memories of that particular topic. Consequently, one Sunday afternoon, I paid him what proved to be the first of a long succession of visits. There I would sit listening to that quiet, unassuming man as he recalled memories of his early life – memories of what seemed like another world.

Eddie was, in the nicest sense of the word, an 'ordinary' man. Not for him would there be fame or fortune; never was his name likely to hit the headlines. But he was one of nature's gentlemen. He had a strong sense of what was right and proper in life, and he lived each day accordingly, even down to the smallest detail. Never once in all our meetings did I see him dressed other than in a smart suit with collar and tie. Every single day he unfailingly dusted his flat, and regularly, once a week, he would give it 'a good go through'. When advancing years made it necessary for him to receive help with his cooking and cleaning, he yielded to pressure from his advisers, but not without registering a protest – he just didn't want to be a nuisance to anybody!

William Edgar Codling, to give him his full name, was a West Norfolk boy, born in 1899 in Hillington, almost in the shadow of Sandringham House. There were very few attractive prospects for the youngsters of those days when they left school and set out to make their way in the world. Quite a number of the boys took the King's shilling and went off to serve their country in the armed forces; for the rest it was work on the land. For most of the girls the only prospect was life in service, either with one of the many landed families in West Norfolk or, for the fortunate few, in the Royal household. It was at this point in his life that fortune smiled on Eddie Codling and he became an under-gardener in the grounds of Sandringham House.

In this situation he was answerable to the Head Gardener, Mr. Cook, and it took that gentleman very little time to discover that he had under his wing a conscientious and trustworthy young lad. Hence, for much of the time, Eddie was left to his own devices – he knew which jobs needed doing and he simply got on with them. It was the time when the widowed Queen Alexandra was still living in Sandringham House, with King George V and Queen Mary occupying York Cottage.

One day, as Eddie was working near York Cottage, there began what he described to me as "the most memorable episode of my life in Sandringham Gardens". As he worked, he was joined by Prince John, the youngest son of King George V and Queen Mary. For half an hour or so the young Prince, then about ten years of age, engaged Eddie in lively conversation before returning to the Cottage. That meeting was, in itself, a memorable event, but what Eddie did not know at the time was that the poor little Prince had been born epileptic.

A few days later, Mr. Cook went to the area where Eddie was working and greeted him with: "Well, Codling, you've certainly

York Cottage at Sandringham.

got a feather in your cap". Eddie, nonplussed, asked for enlightenment.

"Well," said Mr. Cook, "they've asked that you should continue to work around York Cottage so that Prince John can be with you. They think you are such a nice young man".

There was a look of pride on Eddie's face as he told me the story, and one can imagine how he felt when he gave the news to his parents that evening.

From then on, Prince John came out and stayed with him almost every day. Sometimes he would be watching from the window when Eddie arrived for work.

"Wait for me, Ed*ward*," he would shout, always accentuating the second syllable of Eddie's name. "Wait for me!" Then, as the front door banged shut, he would run to help with the day's work.

"He was a lovely little boy," said Eddie. "He was always laughing, and so happy when I let him help me".

But one day, as he was trying to push a wheelbarrow which was much too big for him, he was taken ill and collapsed. Eddie, not knowing what to do, had a feeling of cold panic, but he decided that the best thing to do was to loosen his collar. Then, after a few minutes which seemed an eternity, Prince John announced that he was feeling better and was going indoors.

Some time later, Prince John's governess came from the house

Prince John.

and asked whether anything had happened to John that morning. Eddie told her how he had been taken ill and that he had loosened his collar.

"Well done," she said. "But if ever that happens again, come and call me immediately".

Fortunately, he never had the need to call her.

On another occasion, Eddie decided to row across to the small island in the lake opposite York Cottage to tidy up the rhododendron bushes. Getting a boat from the rustic boathouse, he rowed it to the bank to load up his tools and, just as he was about to push off, he heard the Prince calling: "Don't go, Edward. Wait for me". The little lad ran towards Eddie and got one foot on the boat just as it started to move – then he fell. Luckily, he fell into the boat, but the possible consequences of the Prince falling into the water so unsettled Eddie that he failed to pay sufficient attention to his own well-being. When they made the return trip, he lifted the Prince carefully out onto the safety of the bank – and then he, himself, fell flat on his back into the water. For the Prince, this was the day's culminating delight and he stood on the bank rocking with laughter.

Eventually there came a period when, for several days, Prince John failed to appear. Then, one morning, he came out of York Cottage and walked across to where Eddie was working. Unlike all the previous occasions, he was dressed in a smart little suit.

"Edward," he said. "I am going to London today, so I shall not see you for some time. But look – I have brought you an orange".

After that day, Eddie saw Prince John only once more. The poor little boy died at the age of 14 and was laid to rest in Sandringham Churchyard.

It goes without saying that there was always much to be done in the gardens of Sandringham house, and this was never more so than when the Royal Family were in residence. The packing shed was a hive of industry, with Mr. Cook supervising the provision of flowers for the House and its occupants. Every day saw the arrival in the shed of a number of small, highly polished wooden boxes, each one bearing in gold lettering the name of its owner – King George, Queen Mary and so on. Into each box, lightly packed with tissue paper, was placed a buttonhole or spray of flowers individually produced according to the wishes of the intended wearer. For King George it was always a white carnation with a sprig of maidenhair fern, the stalks neatly wrapped in silver paper. Queen Mary rarely chose anything other than pink carnations, while for Queen Alexandra it was always malmaisons with their gorgeous aroma of cloves.

Then there were the table decorations for dinner – a fresh one every night and always with a seasonal theme. Sometimes there was the dinner table at York Cottage to be decorated as well as that at the House, but quite frequently King George and Queen Mary would walk across the Grounds to join his mother for dinner. Eddie played a part in all this work, and he particularly remembered going through the Gardens with Mr. Cook, each carrying a large basket, seeking out a wide variety of tinted leaves, trails of Virginia Creeper and clutches of red and yellow berries for an autumn display.

Then there was the special floral tribute produced for the funeral of Lady Ffolkes of Hillington Hall. For many years she had been an intimate friend of Queen Alexandra, as well as a great benefactor to the people of Eddie's home village. It added more than a touch of poignancy for him as he helped to fashion the four-foot cross, with maidenhair fern and moss bearing masses of pure white flowers and a centrepiece of white orchids.

Mr. Cook frequently found cause to make use of Eddie Codling's services in yet another capacity – that of chauffeur, although it must be remembered that the various means of transport were all horse-drawn in those days. Whenever he wanted to visit somebody in the locality, Eddie would drive him there, either in the dog cart or the gig. They were using the latter on one occasion when the journey took them through Eddie's home village, and there he sat, high above his passenger, hoping that one or two of the villagers would be suitably impressed by the sight of Eddie Codling in charge of one of the Royal vehicles. He sat proudly upright, the reins in one hand, the whip poised at the correct angle, and wearing his new bowler hat, coat and gloves. Sadly, however, the roads of Hillington were completely deserted.

There followed another drive when Eddie almost found himself and his vehicle enshrined in the folklore of West Norfolk. It was an occasion when Queen Alexandra was hostess to a large dinner party at Sandringham House and there was a shortage of drivers to return the guests to their homes. Somebody was needed to convey three of the company to Snettisham Hall in the early hours of the morning, and Mr. Cook's thoughts immediately turned to

Eddie. Eddie, eager to oblige, tried to ignore two lingering doubts which the prospect raised in his mind – firstly, his experience of night driving was limited to one or two trips with his father's pony; secondly, and even more disconcertingly, the fact that there were to be three passengers meant that the dog cart would not be suitable – it had to be a closed-in brougham, a vehicle he had never driven. But he kept his doubts to himself and eagerly awaited the experience.

Although nobody would see him in the darkness of the night, he felt a surge of pride as he donned his coat, gloves and bowler hat and harnessed his horse to the brougham. It was a four-wheeled vehicle with a door at the back and iron steps to enable the passengers to enter. Inside there were padded leather seats which would comfortably accommodate four people, and a small window which opened near the coachman's box and through which instructions could be given to the driver.

The Norwich Gates stood open, flanked on one side by a police sergeant and on the other by a constable. Eddie climbed up on to the driver's box and, within a few minutes, the signal came for him to take his vehicle to the door of the House. He drove round and under the portico and, in the brightly-lit hall, he could see his passengers saying their farewells to Her Majesty. Footmen escorted them to the waiting brougham and, when they were comfortably seated, Eddie started on his journey. Through the Gates they went, sent on their way with a smart salute from the police sergeant, and Eddie could hardly believe what he was doing. Was he really driving one of the Royal carriages through those splendid Norwich Gates, or was it all a dream?

But there was no time to dwell on the matter, for the tall trees loomed dark and ominous on either side of the road and, as he came to the top of the notorious Dersingham Hill, Eddie was already having misgivings as to how the horse would react. He took no chances. A touch on the hand brake, a slowing down to walking pace – and then a sigh of relief as they rounded the corner by Parker's Shop. The rest was plain sailing. Off with the brake, and the horse broke into a steady trot as they passed through Dersingham and Ingoldisthorpe. Then came the approach to Snettisham Hall, the gates of its walled Park already open and the front door illuminated by a single lamp. Eddie brought the brougham to a halt, his passengers alighted and off he went on his return trip to Sandringham.

It was a late autumn night and Eddie had only travelled a few hundred yards when he suddenly realised how cold it was.

"What a chump I am," he thought, "sitting up here when I could be much more comfortable inside".

Almost immediately the thought was transferred into action. He stopped the brougham and, opening the little window, passed the reins through, climbed inside and closed the door. This was fine – much better than being perched up there on that old box. It needed only a word of encouragement to the horse, whose instinct told her she was on her way home, and off they went, jogging along at a steady pace.

All went well until they were negotiating the S-bend leaving Snettisham, when a loud shout suddenly pierced the stillness of the night: "Whoa! Whoa!"

Eddie stopped the horse, opened the door and looked out to see the source of the shout. There, in the light from the carriage lamps, stood the figure of the village policeman, leaning on his bicycle and with his mouth hanging open in amazement.

"What's the matter?" asked Eddie.

The constable took off his helmet, scratched his head and gasped: "Well, bless my soul! I thought that old hoss must be runnin' away or suffin' when I din't see nobody a-drivin' on it".

The expression on his face told the whole story – he thought he had come across "The Phantom Coach of Snettisham"!

Memorable though they were, Eddie's early years in the gardens at Sandringham were just the prologue to a long and varied life that lay ahead. Before long he was to don a soldier's uniform and to be wounded while fighting in France with the Rifle Brigade. Then, on his return to Norfolk, he was to meet and marry Flo, with whom he took over the management of a refreshment stall on Norwich Market Place. They were a devoted couple and were happy serving their customers for more than 45 years until their retirement in 1965. Then, in 1986, Flo died and Eddie was left alone with his memories. It was then that I first met him and, all the while, his thoughts went back to those happy days on the Royal Estate and, in particular, to one person – Queen Alexandra.

Just as Edward VII became known as "The Peacemaker", so Alexandra was affectionately regarded by all who knew her as a great benefactor, and Eddie was always ready to recall her many kindnesses.

Eddie Codling: The young soldier and the happy pensioner

There was the day when one of the stable lads fell from his horse with a fatal heart attack. Knowing that his mother was a widow and in failing health, Alexandra paid the funeral expenses and not only awarded her a pension but also arranged for her to be sent to a London hospital for treatment. Then, on her return, she paid frequent visits to the widow's little cottage, where she would sit and read to her.

Queen Alexandra would also visit the hospital in Bloomsbury which bore her name. There she would go from ward to ward, speaking to each of the young patients and leaving little presents of sweets and toys. Eddie particularly liked recalling how one tiny patient, attracted by the sweet, smiling face above her cot, impulsively put her arms round the Queen's neck and kissed her.

Queen Alexandra took a great personal interest in Sir Ernest Shackleton's explorations of the south polar regions. In December, 1914 he had set sail from South Georgia in the *Endurance* but, within a few weeks, the ship became trapped and crushed by ice. The party set up camp on the ice, where they were to be marooned until their eventual rescue in April, 1916. The expedition was much overshadowed by the Great War, and no news had been received during all those long months of imprisonment on the ice.

When news of Shackleton's disastrous failure reached England,

Alexandra was among the first to send a message of condolence. Then, on his return, she invited him to Sandringham, where she persuaded him to give a slide show and talk about his ill-fated expedition. Invitations went out to the Queen's many friends all over Norfolk, as well as to members of the Estate staff – and Eddie was one of the lucky ones.

The audience had received instructions to assemble in the ballroom half an hour before the start of the talk, and Eddie was pleased to find that his seat was quite near the large white doors through which the Royal party would enter. On either side of these doors stood a footman, resplendent in immaculate breeches, black patent shoes, scarlet and gold trimmed jacket and powdered wig. When all were assembled, an equerry entered, spraying disinfectant into the air all along the aisle – a necessary precaution, for the country was in the grip of a flu epidemic.

Then came the great moment as the doors opened wide and Queen Alexandra, accompanied by a lady-in-waiting, entered the ballroom. Wearing a shimmering white gown and diamond tiara, she made her way to her seat, smiling here and there as she recognised a familiar face. Then the lights were lowered and Shackleton began his story of his expedition's long and arduous imprisonment on the antarctic ice. He held his listeners spellbound until, all too soon, the lights came on and the entertainment was over. Queen Alexandra slowly rose from her seat and proceeded to leave the ballroom, with every member of the audience standing and bowing as she passed. The footmen opened the doors and then, as she reached Eddie, she paused to ask if he had enjoyed it.

"Yes, thank you, Your Majesty," said Eddie.

"Yes," said the Queen, "it really was thrilling, wasn't it?"

With that, she turned towards the doors, which closed softly behind her.

"Those few words," said Eddie, "were the climax of a truly wonderful afternoon – a memory that will stay with me for the rest of my days".

I enjoyed Eddie's friendship – and his memories – for just five short years. Then, on September 11th, 1994, only a few weeks from his 95th birthday, he breathed his last – it would be wrong to say that he died for, like the old soldier that he was, he simply faded away. He left this life in the way that he had always lived it – quietly and in complete peace. A truly gentle man.

CHAPTER 15

Making Music.

One of the great disappointments of my life has been my inability to produce music in any shape or form. I was never taught to play a man-made instrument, nor have I ever been able to use the diaphragm and vocal chords with which the Almighty endowed me to produce a musical sound which would fall pleasurably on a listener's ear.

In my own defence, I can only plead that it is all a matter of genes, for I come from a very non-musical family. The tradition of family songs around the piano, still popular with some of our acquaintances in my early boyhood, was not for us. Any such concerted effort on our part would surely have brought forth complaints from the neighbours and sent our Airedale, Bonzo, diving for cover. It was not that we had no liking for music. We had a wind-up gramophone and a wide selection of records which were played over and over again until the grooves were almost worn flat. No – it was just that we couldn't sing in tune.

Furthermore, my yearning for a good singing voice was not stimulated by any desire on my part to be a performer – I simply wanted to be able to join in with the others. Never do I feel that yearning more strongly than when I am in a church congregation. I start off with the best of intentions, determined to sing my heart out, but then it happens. It matters not in which church I find myself, nor where I stand among the congregation. I open my mouth in eager readiness to give of my best – but then I am thwarted. Every time, with heart-breaking regularity, standing just a few feet from me is a woman who obviously harbours a strong belief that she could be an operatic prima donna. Her voice drowns all others in our corner of the church, and my faint offering is strangled at birth. I have no option other than to fall back on my only alternative – that of mime.

Now, miming is something at which I really can claim many years of great success. It all began in the thirties, when I was a young lad at North Walsham Council School. Our headmaster, Mr. Colthorpe, was very proud of the School Choir, with which he spent many long hours in his battle for perfection. All his efforts were geared to a certain date in the calendar – the day on which his seventy or eighty choristers would make the journey to Norwich to compete in the Schools Music Festival at St. Andrew's Hall. He was determined that his choir should win as many classes as possible and, every year, he and his boys would return home at the end of the day, proudly bearing the banners which indicated that they had not let him down.

At every festival, the biggest threat came from the youngsters of Southery School, which had a very high reputation in the musical life of Norfolk at that time. We, in North Walsham, had only a vague idea of where Southery was. We knew it was somewhere in the west of the county, probably not far from King's Lynn, but in those days of limited travel it might just as well have been on the other side of the world. But one thing was certain – if our choir was to win, Southery had to be beaten. It was on that target that Mr. Colthorpe set his sights, and his young singers got down to work with a feverish intensity.

In the circumstances, with so much tension and such a lot at stake, it may seem strange that I, with my complete inability to hit more than the occasional note correctly, should want to be a member of the choir. There were two reasons. Firstly, all the other boys were there and I had no wish to be left out; and then there was the trip to Norwich which, in itself, made it a red-letter day. I therefore hatched my fiendish plot – I would mime it all. I suppose I can now claim to have mimed to the music of one of the biggest backing groups ever assembled, but we didn't call it miming in those days – just 'pretend-singing'.

As I look back on the event, I wonder how on earth I managed to hoodwink both Mr. Colthorpe and the adjudicators, but I did it, and the choir was successful. At the end of the day we returned to North Walsham and, with our banners held aloft, paraded through the Market Place to the applause of the assembled townsfolk.

Amongst my present-day friends there are those who, only too well aware of my musical disability, seem to harbour certain doubts concerning the veracity of my story. There is, however, recorded proof for, at the end of the Festival, the choir assembled at the side of St. Andrew's Hall for a group photograph. In the bottom right-hand corner of that group, with a mop of fair hair and no cap, is the little boy who couldn't sing a note to save his life – and nobody ever knew!

North Walsham Council School Choir, c.1929.

The feeling of euphoria which accompanied our Festival success lasted for a full week. Then, as I made my way across the Market Place on my way home from school, it dissolved with all the immediacy of a snowflake falling upon the flames of a bonfire. The reason for the sudden change in my mental state was the sight of John Dixon walking in my direction with the obvious intention of speaking to me.

Now, Mr. Dixon was a pillar of North Walsham society – not the kind of person with whom, at my tender age, I was accustomed to having casual conversations. An auctioneer and estate agent by profession, he was also Clerk to the local Pension Committee, Deputy Registrar of Smallburgh district, and Chairman of the town's bench of magistrates. More significantly, however, he was also organist and choirmaster at the Parish Church.

"Hold on there, young Bagshaw," he said.

I stopped dead in my tracks, wondering why this important man should want to have words with me.

"They tell me you were one of the boys who won the banners last week," he said. "How would you like to come and sing in the Church Choir?"

I froze, both mentally and physically. It seemed an eternity before I fell back on the age-old answer so beloved by all small boys when faced with an awkward situation.

"I don't know," I replied.

"You'd enjoy it," he said. "And you get a tip for weddings". Money was the last thing on my mind.

"I don't know," I repeated.

"Well, give it a bit of thought," said Mr. Dixon. "I'll have a word with your father about it".

For the next few days the matter was never far from my mind, but I need not have worried. Whether or not he spoke to my father I shall never know, but I heard no more about it. In truth, I would dearly have loved to join the Church Choir, for it included a number of my schoolmates among its ranks. Yet I knew I would be flirting with disaster if I attempted to continue my miming act in such a situation.

By the time I went to grammar school I realised that life would be easier if I faced up to my musical disability and admitted that I just could not sing. This was brought home to me even more by the fact that, in my Form at Paston, there were two boys who had the most beautiful treble voices I had ever heard. Whether in solos

The Choir of North Walsham Parish Church (John Dixon, with moustache, sits next to the Vicar) – they never knew how near they came to disaster!

136

or duets, Randolph Bacon and Jack Points could have charmed the very birds out of the trees. Compared to those two lads I was, quite simply, a non-runner.

It was at that stage in our careers that we in Form IIa came under the musical tutelage of that doyen of the North Norfolk musical scene, Norman Cutting. I struggled manfully through his periods of instruction, and they passed by without any great incident of note (Please forgive the unintentional pun!). Then, however, came the day when, completely without prior warning, he decided to investigate the individual singing skills of his charges. He proposed to do this by lining us up in two rows and, while we sang selections from the usual schoolboy repertoire of that era, he would pass slowly along behind the rows, listening carefully to each boy in turn. I decided this was too much. Up went my hand.

"Please, Sir. Can I be excused?"

"Excused?" said Mr. Cutting. "For what reason?"

"Because I can't sing, Sir," I replied.

"Can't sing?" he said. "Nonsense! Everybody can sing!"

I knew this was by no means a true statement of fact, but I had no alternative other than to take my place in line.

I am not sure which ballads received our treatment that day, but I think we had dealt with *The Ash Grove* and were just having a stab at *Danny Boy* when I felt his presence behind me. The seconds which followed were nothing less than mental torture, but I tried my hardest and, to be quite honest, I thought I was doing rather well. Then, however, I felt a tap on my shoulder, and Mr. Cutting spoke:

"You're quite right," he said. "You CAN'T sing!"

Of course, liking music and being musical are two very different things. To have an 'ear' for music, you have to be born with it. I am sure it is something which cannot be taught. Sadly, I was born without it. So, also, was little Lucilla Reeve, who grew up at the turn of the century in the Breckland village of Tottington. Yet her musical success far outshone mine, for she learned to play both the piano and the organ – after a fashion.

She had no desire to learn music, but it was a time when children did as they were told. She tried her hardest to achieve a degree of proficiency with both instruments, but it was all a struggle, and the situation was not helped by her mother's choice of tutor. The village boasted two music teachers, and it was

Tottington School, where Lucilla Reeve practiced
on the piano and the American Organ.

unfortunate for Lucilla that hers was to be the schoolmistress, for
the two of them shared a mutual dislike for each other. "Staying
behind for a music lesson," she said, "was almost as bad as being
kept in after school to re-do a puckered seam".

The organ on which she practised was an instrument known as
an American Organ, much in favour at the time and regarded as
being a step above the harmonium. Such organs were rather bulky
and very ornate – ideal for accommodating the vast array of bric-
a-brac with which the Victorians so loved to clutter their front
parlours. Indeed, in some homes the American Organ was acquired
simply as a handsome piece of furniture – if somebody later
learned to play the thing it was regarded as something of a bonus.

When Lucilla presented herself for her music lessons she never
knew on which instrument she would be required to perform. If
the schoolmistress and her assistant were having a cooked meal it
would be the piano in the schoolroom. If they were having
afternoon tea it would be the organ in the parlour while they
partook of their tea and cakes. This instrument was adorned with
ornaments and vases of dried grasses – and metal-framed
photographs of the family who looked down upon Lucilla,
seemingly with an air of contempt, as she struggled through her
pieces. They were presumably musical!

It was a small room and, for the duration of her lesson, it became filled with such a babel of assorted sounds as to be almost unbearable. There was the rattle of the impedimenta on the organ, the clatter of the teacups and the chatter of the teachers. Then, as Lucilla tried to use her feet to muster up sufficient wind to see her through *The Blue Bells of Scotland,* it seemed that the very walls of the room were in danger of being burst asunder. On one occasion, when she was blundering through a march, she pulled out two stops by mistake, and the resultant loud blast so shook the instrument that a framed, bearded gentleman, as well as a vase of grasses, crashed to the carpet. Two shillings for the vase was added to the bill for the next lesson and, soon after that disaster, she was considered sufficiently proficient not to need any further lessons.

Although she never really cared about music, Lucilla did try her best to be able to play properly, even to the extent of getting up at 7 o'clock on summer mornings for two hours' practice. She confesses to never having completely mastered it, but she did reach a high enough standard to play for church services. Her biggest problem was something to do with not letting your right hand know what your left hand is doing, for, while she played the treble part without mistake, her left hand would be giving its own version of the bass. Strangely enough, nobody else seemed to notice this deficiency and, as time went on, she began more and more to ignore the written music for the left hand and make it up as she went along! Still nobody noticed – until she was asked to play the organ in a nearby village one winter when the organist was ill.

She had performed her duties there before and managed the usual chants and hymns without incident, but this was to be a special occasion, with one carol being sung by the choir alone. The Christmas decorations had been left in place, hiding the organ from the choir, and, as things turned out, this proved to be a blessing in disguise. What Lucilla did not know was that the leader of the choir, newly promoted to surplices and feeling very important, was proud of his bass voice, and all his relations were there to hear him sing.

The service took place and, as far as Lucilla was aware, everything had gone well. It was not until the congregation had filed out and she heard the sound of heavy footsteps coming up the church to where she was gathering up her books ready for the five-mile cycle ride home that she realised that something was amiss. Suddenly, round the organ screen, there appeared a very angry man – the newly-promoted leader of the choir. His face was red, the ends of his moustache had become unwaxed and the oiled curl which should have been adorning his forehead hung limply down over one eye. He was almost too angry to speak, but suddenly he burst forth. She might have come from away, he said, and thought she could play the organ but her playing had ruined his bass part which all his relations had come to hear.

It was only the arrival of the very nervous Vicar which stopped his flow of words and gave Lucilla the chance to pour oil on troubled waters. Unfortunately, it turned out to be petrol for, when she hurriedly said that the sheer beauty of his singing had so captivated her that she had been unable to play properly, he nearly exploded. Her playing of the bass part was so bad, he said, that he had been unable to sing a single note!

She retired suitably crestfallen, leaving the Vicar to make the best of the situation. She was never asked to take duty there again, a situation which suited her admirably.

CHAPTER 16

Charles Loynes Smith.

I think it might well come as a surprise to many people to hear of a man working for fifty years as a blacksmith without ever shoeing a horse or even making a shoe; but Charles Loynes Smith was one such man. Though he spent his entire working life fashioning metal with the dedicated skill of a craftsman, he never came in direct contact with a horse, except when helping at harvest time on his relatives' farm at Hethersett. His skills lay in other directions and now, nearly half a century after his passing, evidence of the work of his hands can be found all around us.

Chas. L. Smith was born in 1880 and, at the age of 15, was apprenticed to a Hethersett coachbuilder who had a nationwide reputation as a builder of two-wheeled horse-drawn vehicles. That man was William Wade of Queens Road in the village, and his speciality was governess carts. Young Charles spent the first year of his apprenticeship as mate and striker to an older apprentice, working a 60-hour week for a wage of three shillings. In his second year he carried out the same duties, but as mate to the head smith, Harry Watling, who encouraged him to work at the forge when he himself was away from it. William Wade was also a great encourager of boys, and he offered a bonus of a shilling a dozen for small repetitive items such as wing stays. Charles' weekly wage had risen to four shillings, but he was sometimes able to earn as much as two shillings extra by filling odd minutes in that way.

During his third year he worked regularly at the forge, with a younger boy as striker, making ironwork for governess carts. He was now 17 and was paid six shillings a week, with occasional overtime at twopence an hour. His fourth and final year, during which he reached his 19th birthday, saw his wages increase to eight shillings, and he was then capable of making any piece of ironwork for a cart, as well as forging and tempering springs, and shoeing wheels with iron or steel tyres.

At the end of his apprenticeship he stayed with William Wade for a few months as an 'improver' before moving on to a new situation in Norwich. This was with the renowned coachbuilder, Charles Thorn, at St. Giles' Gates, where he received £1 per week. He lodged in Rupert Street, paying nine shillings a week for 'bed, board and attendance' and going home to Hethersett for weekends.

"At Thorn's," he later said, "I saw the finest craftsmen in iron I have ever seen. They made fore-carriages, edge-plates, pump handles and all the intricate work for broughams, landaus, victorias and the like, and their rate was sixpence an hour for a 60-hour week. I despaired of ever attaining their skill and proficiency," he added, "but, before I had a chance to try, all that kind of work was relegated to the museums by the advent of the motor car".

In August 1900 the lure of London enticed him to go and work for a firm that built everything from omnibuses to bread vans and from coal wagons to milk lorries. It was all heavier and coarser work, with nothing approaching the fine craftsmanship of the men he had left behind in Norwich, but the pay was good – £2 for a 56-hour week. He paid fourteen shillings a week for board and lodgings, saved £20 in 20 weeks, sent for his Norfolk sweetheart and got married. He worked in London for five years in an underground smith's shop, lit only by a gas flame, and then moved on to High Wycombe where, through the open smithy doors, he could see the wide expanse of greensward known as 'The Rye Mead'. There he took a cut of five shillings a week in his wages, but the cost of living was considerably lower than in London, and he stayed for four years.

All the while, the call back to his Norfolk roots became stronger and more difficult to resist. Then, in 1909, his young wife died after just nine years of marriage, leaving him with three young children. It was now a matter of necessity that he should return to Norfolk, where he knew that he would have the support of his sister. She had married into the farming family Richardson at Hethersett, and he felt that his home village had much more to offer than the lonely surroundings of Buckinghamshire.

So it was back to Hethersett, where he had to adapt himself to yet more new techniques, for his work was now concerned with agricultural machinery – ploughs, drills, chaff-cutters and the like. For four successive winters he spent 16 weeks making 'L' hoes by hand and, by working steadily for a week of 60 hours, he could make eight dozen, for which he was paid five shillings a dozen. "This," he said, "was the hardest physical toil I ever did, for the iron and steel blades had to be beaten out to a knife edge, and each blow was like hitting the face of the anvil".

In 1913 he once more returned to work in Norwich, this time for a firm of constructional engineers and suppliers of general ironwork for the building trade. Here again a fresh technique had to be acquired, working to architectural drawings and blueprints. He worked for that firm for just two years, but he left behind a number of lasting memorials to his skill. All the forged work on the gates of Britannia Barracks came from his hands, as did the wrought numbers and wall ties at Stuart Court in Recorder Road and the door hinges at St. Luke's Church in Aylsham Road – not to mention the huge iron framework above the entrance to the South Pier at Lowestoft.

In 1915 he moved to another Norwich firm, where he was to stay for the last thirty years of his working life. Here, all the various techniques he had learned over the years were called into use, for they were 'general' smiths. During the last five years he was largely occupied in doing what he had learned to do in his early years – forging and tempering road springs. Now, however, they were not needed for governess carts and broughams, for another war had broken out and they were destined for use on military vehicles.

Then, in 1945, came his retirement. "My motto in life," he said, "has always been 'Something attempted, something done', and now that belief has earned me a little repose. So, as my reward for fifty years of ungrudging service is ten shillings a week contributory pension, I propose to take it".

Thus, he put aside the tools of his trade, but he could look across the face of the city he loved and see a wealth of testimony to the skill of his hands: the curtain rods round the high altar in Norwich Cathedral, every inch of which bears the marks of his hammer to make them look old; the exterior and interior hinges of St. Alban's Church at Lakenham, as well as the wrought iron frame of the west window; the Gothic panels to the headmaster's desk in the Grammar School Chapel; the bracketing supporting the figures of the Virgin and Child in St. John's, Timberhill; and the balustrades to the stairs at St. Crispin's Hall in Pitt Street.

One might well consider such a list to be a fitting memorial to one person's life, but C.L. Smith was a man of many parts and he left his mark in a variety of ways. Besides being a craftsman with his hands, he was also a man of brilliant and incisive intellect.

Although he left school at the age of fourteen, he was widely read in the classics and had a great love of poetry. A fine preacher and public speaker, he could also talk knowledgeably on economic and political subjects, and it was those talents which were to stand him in good stead when, in his retirement, he was elected to Norwich City Council.

He was a member of the Housing Committee in 1950 when new housing estates were being built in Lakenham and Earlham, as well as private housing on the site adjoining Eaton Road. The developments involved the construction of a number of new roads, and a sub-committee was called upon to recommend suitable names for them. That sub-committee consisted of just one man – C.L. Smith – and his recommendations were accepted in their entirety.

Charles Smith had firm views on the selection of street names. They should, he believed, be easy to pronounce, they should not bear any similarity to existing names and, wherever possible, they should have some sort of local association. To help him in his task he took himself off to the Public Library and armed himself with two books – Blomefield's *Norfolk* of 1741 and a book by Walter Rye.

The Sandy Lane – Cooper Lane Estate is in Lakenham, so he quite naturally turned to what Blomefield records about that district. He searched through the list of vicars of the parish from 1308 onwards and, having rejected many of the earlier ones, he selected the surname of John **Harwood,** who had been the Vicar in 1666. From there he turned his attention to churches to pick out the name **Theobald.** There was, according to Blomefield, an image of St. Theobald which attracted many pilgrims to the church of St. John the Baptist. The third name, **Coleburn,** was that of a priest who founded a chapel in Lakenham at the time of the Norman Conquest, while the final one, **Berkley,** is derived from George, Lord Berkley, who was Lord of the Manor in 1640.

The Woodlands Estate is in Earlham, so the one-man sub-committee again searched through the list of vicars. Avoiding such names as Shinkill, he found three pleasant names all beginning with the same initial letter as the estate itself. Thus, the new residents were obliged for three new street names to Will **Winchcomb** (1464), Nic **Waterman** (1470) and Richard **Wheatley** (1526).

For the private development adjoining Eaton Road just two

names were needed and, for these, Mr. Smith culled **Welsford** and **Lyhart** from Walter Rye's *Monographs of Norwich Hamlets.* George Day, a 19th century Vicar of Eaton, had a son named Welsford who died at sea at the age of 17 – a rather tenuous connection, but gratefully seized upon. For the final name a relationship was established between Eaton and the celebrated Bishop Walter Lyhart, who was responsible for the fine vaulted roof of the nave of Norwich Cathedral and is so often mentioned in the Paston Letters.

Those, then, were the names accepted by Norwich City Council at their meeting in April 1950. What a wealth of meaning they carry – so much more satisfying than Bramble Lane or Heather Close!

But C.L. Smith had yet another talent. For years he took great delight in penning pieces of local prose and blank verse – the latter in the Norfolk idiom – and, every week, his writings appeared in the local Press under the heading of A Norfolk Miscellany. To lovers of Norfolk it was all sheer delight, and I am happy to be able to include one of my favourite pieces of his work:

Ol' Punch Hoss.

He wornt ezzackly a pritty hoss,
But, my heart, he could pull a load.
He must ha' weighed thatty hunderdweight.
He'd got a gret long ugly old hid
Werry near as big as a wheelbarrer.
He was a sort er datty black
And his old coat was as rough
As the hind part of a porkypine.
He had two gret old hind legs
What might ha' belonged to a nellerfant.
As orkard an ol' bit o' hossflesh
As ever put his hid tru a collar.
He wanted a quarter an acre to tahn round in,
An' you coont back him two yards
Cause he was so stiff in the jints.
But goin' forrard – he'd pull anything.
He woont never jib at nothin',
He'd ha' shifted the Rock o' Giberaltar.

Elliott's chaps were shiftin' a troshin' ingin.
That may fare funny to you.
Movin' troshin' tackle wi' hosses,
But thass what we had ter du then.
They'd got a couple o' hosses on the drum,
An' that was sunk in an inch or two.
Well, bor, they kep' pamplin' about
Like a couple o' cats on hot bricks.
They kep' hullin' theirselves on the traices
An' then goin' backards agin.
I thowt they'd ha' busted the harness.
They'd never ha' shifted th' old drum.
They woont pull an ol' hin off the nest.
I say "Take you yar two annermals orf.
I'll show you how ter shift that there drum".
Thass as true as I set here, bor,
I arn't tellin' a wahd of a lie.
I hung Ol' Punch on that there drum.
I say "Come on ol' feller, stiddy now".
He jest give a sorter grunt an' a groan
An' eased his weight inter th' collar
An' out that ol' drum came
As if that was a pramberlater.
Ah, poor ol' Punch.
He was a nugly, orkard ol' warmin.
But, my heart, he could wholly pull.

Charles Loynes Smith died in 1952 at the age of 72. Throughout the years he had trodden faithfully in the footsteps of his father, whose Christian names he had inherited and who, also, was a first-class blacksmith and a man of sterling character. There can be little doubt that he had led a full life, always fortified by his strong Christian Faith.

In his boyhood he had witnessed the misery brought about by over-indulgence in alcohol, and he steadfastly made up his mind that he would never touch a drop of the stuff. He kept his vow to the very end. As he lay on his death bed in hospital, somebody offered him a small tot of brandy. He quietly declined.

"I've done without it all these years," he said. "I don't intend to start now".

5

Visitors

There's the wind on the heath, brother;
if I could only feel that,
I would gladly live for ever.

George Borrow, *Lavengro*, 1851.

CHAPTER 17

The Road To Nowhere.

We're on the road to nowhere; everyone passes by.
Nobody comes to Norfolk unless there's a reason why.

That little childhood jingle, which we used to recite with more than a little pride and pleasure, contained a fair element of truth, for there were times when visitors to Norfolk were few and far between. It also helps to explain our traditional hesitancy in accepting newcomers, for the sudden appearance of strangers in our midst was historically a reason for suspicion. It all stemmed from the last five words of the jingle – the reason why they had come.

After all, the Romans had come for a reason. They wanted to extend their empire, and just think of the trouble and hardship their presence brought to the locals. Then there were the Anglo-Saxons who landed along our county's northern coastline and became the dominant strain in our long, mixed ancestry. Their arrival was cursed by the Romans who, history tells us, continually found it necessary to march and counter-march their glittering, dusty cohorts from Brancaster to repel their unpredictable, turbulent invasions.

When the Romans finally withdrew, the Anglo-Saxons came in force and seized the land which still bears their name – the North-folk and the South-folk. They came like the wind out of the cold North Sea, bringing the sea, which was their natural home, into our county, so that sea and land were to remain forever jointly our heritage. It was not by mere chance that Nelson was born on that coastline!

They came to our shores as flaxen-haired, pestilent barbarians, but they, like the Romans, had a reason for colonising our land. One could, in fact, say that their reason was the more justifiable, for they had been driven from their natural homeland on the desolate coasts and windswept mud-flats of Germany and Denmark. They had become men of the ocean, pirates of the sea, sailing their curved long-boats to wherever they could find succour and sustenance. Because of the nature of their existence, they were also barbaric savages, prepared to slaughter and destroy as they sailed the watery wastes, rather like wild geese, in their search for a permanent home. Yet, when they settled in our land and became its permanent residents, they brought a kind of life which was to endure and far transcend their own simple beginnings – a life which was to imbue their descendants, even to the present day, with three great passions.

Firstly there was their attitude to the sea which skirts so much of our county boundary. They were great seamen, and Norfolk men have inherited the ability to work with the ocean rather than to fear it as an enemy. Then there was their constant searching for freedom in all its forms – and we, today, still delight in indulging in the freedom to 'dew different', even if others may consider us slightly eccentric in some of our activities. Finally, the Anglo-Saxons loved the soil and the tending of it and its beasts. Bronze Age men left their memorial in burial grounds; the Romans in stone; but our true ancestors left theirs in the imperishable shape of the earth they tilled. It is written large across our county, with their villages and farms, their meadows and their ploughlands.

Once things in Norfolk had settled down and invasions by sea had become things of the past, visitors became very few and far between. The county was pretty well isolated from the rest of the country by its geographical boundaries – the sea, the Wash, the Fens, the rivers and the Brecks; and the road system, such as it was, was not conducive to long-distance travelling. The fact that many countryfolk worked in solitary fashion, whether on land or sea, also led to a marked degree of aloofness and made them, as they themselves put it, "timid wi' strangers". An old countryman of my acquaintance had his own way of describing the situation:

"Dew a foreigner come along," he said, "we don't say nawthen. We just go on our way. We wait an' see how he turn out. We like to summer an' winter 'em fust".

One of the great fears has always been that the incomer might want to change things, and Norfolk folk simply cannot abide change. Many years ago, the Reverend Harold Fitch told of how a colleague of his put a really beautiful stained-glass window in his church. The people disliked it (or, at any rate, the idea of it), but they "didn't say nawthen" until one old man could contain his feelings no longer.

"I don't hold wi' these hare painted winders," he said. "Why can't we keep the plain glass, as God Almighty made it?"

Newly-appointed parsons frequently came up against the wrath of their parishioners when they acted in too great haste in making changes in church matters. It must be remembered that there was a great social and educational divide between the rector and most members of his congregation. The countryman was highly-skilled in matters concerning the land, but there his knowledge ended. The parson, on the other hand, was endowed with all the knowledge, both temporal and spiritual, which went with an honours degree from Oxford or Cambridge. Canon Marcon, Rector of Edgefield from 1876 to 1937, expressed his feelings on taking up his appointment thus: "Coming as a young man from a curacy in the West of England and not so long after the sweet camaraderie of College life – so full of animation and vigorous thought – I found life amongst bucolics very slow and lonely".

He went on to describe an incident concerning 'Mr. Brummell, the Rector of Holt up to about 1900, a most punctual man, and probably one of the finest mathematicians who ever passed through Cambridge'. Mr. Brummell had only just been appointed Rector, and he was introducing a few alterations in the services of the church which were not appreciated by his Clerk, a man named Beresford. At first Mr. Beresford "didn't say nawthen", but before long it was more than he could stand and he accosted Mr. Brummell in forthright Norfolk manner:

"Now look yew here, Rector! If you mearke any more of these changes in Church, I tell yew what I'll do – I'm blowed if I oont hull the job up!"

The gentle, very learned Don, fresh from Cambridge, was quite taken aback but, recovering his equilibrium, he said, "Come now, Mr. Beresford, pray what do you mean by 'hulling it up'?"

"What?" replied the Clerk. "Yew a larned man, come from College, and yew don't know what 'hullin' on it up' means. I'm ashamed on yer!" and, turning on his heel, he strode off, leaving the poor Rector dumbfounded.

The fact that not many visitors came to Norfolk before the building of the railways is mirrored in the similar fact that not many Norfolk people themselves went travelling. For those with both the need and the money there were horse-drawn coaches rattling along the turnpikes, but the county's earlier generations were a fairly static breed. I suppose today's youngsters may well have a slight feeling of disbelief that a person could live to the age of 100 without ever venturing outside the county, but such was the case. Even stranger is the fact that, in the time of our grandparents, many Norfolk countryfolk never ventured more than a few miles from their home parish. The simple reason is that they never found the need to go further and the limit of their travel was dictated by how far they could walk. A horse or a bicycle widened their horizons whilst, for such people as the country housewife with eggs and butter to take to market, there was always the chance of getting a lift on the carrier's cart. But they were not great travellers in those days.

A former Rector of Edgefield used to tell how he met one of his old parishioners walking along the road to the village with another old man who was unknown to him.

"And who's your friend?" he said.

"Thass my brother," replied the man. "Thass the first time I ha' seen him for several years, 'cause he've been away".

"Where has he been?" said the Rector, thinking of Australia or America.

"He've been at Briston," said the old man.

As Briston is only about a couple of miles away, the Rector was unable to suppress a smile, which did not please the old man.

"Oh, no," he said. "He ha'nt been at Briston all the time – he were at Hunworth afore that".

Neither of the parishes was more than two miles from Edgefield!

So the countryfolk went about their business in splendid isolation, quite happy to continue Norfolk's role as the Granary of England. The loneliness of their working lives was well illustrated by J.H.B. Peel, one of the greatest of countryside writers and also, incidentally, son of the popular wireless comedian of the thirties, Gillie Potter. He spent a splendid summer day walking the byways of Norfolk and then went home and 'wrote us up' for the *Daily Telegraph:*

"Two cuckoos called a time of year and, when one of them stopped, the other answered its own echo. Small hills carried little woods which harboured blackbird and chiff-chaff and robin and wren, all whistling while they worked. Noticing a distant scarecrow, I blinked because the heat haze gave the effigy the power to sway. Closer inspection showed that the metronome was a man, hoeing a leguminous ocean".

By some miracle of fortune, East Anglia played no part in the Industrial Revolution which marred so much of England. Industry regarded the region as a backwater, though it was eager enough to be fed by its farmers. But then came the railways and, when sleepy little Melton Constable became Norfolk's Crewe, the rest of Britain soon realised that there was more to be seen in our rural backwater than just a collection of straw-chewing yokels, even though we were 'on the road to nowhere'.

Cromer, of course, gave up being just a sleepy little fishing village and built a string of hotels and streets of boarding houses to accommodate the visitors. They came to enjoy the sea, the sand and the champagne-like quality of the air, and Cromer was never the same again, for a new industry had been born. Clement Scott, another of the *Telegraph* writers, wrote about the charms of the area, although it was Overstrand rather than Cromer that captured his heart. I am not sure whether it was Scott who first gave the area the title of Poppyland, but he it was who fell deeply under the spell of Beckhythe, just along the coast, and penned those much-loved lines about "The Garden of Sleep".

Another writer who was spurred into verse by the delights of the area was Norman Gale, whose poem, "Off To The Sea", was first published in 1907. Here are the first and fourth verses:

Here comes the train! Goodbye, Papa!
Goodbye, goodbye to all!
We'll watch you from the window
Till your bodies grow quite small.
They say the engine flies along
Much faster than a bee.
We're going down to Sheringham
To paddle in the sea!

At Cromer we shall find a man
To drive a wagonette
Past chicory and poppies –
How we hope it won't be wet!
And when we reach our lodgings
We shall quickly have our tea.
We're going down to Sheringham
To paddle in the sea!

On the grass of the cliff, at the edge of the steep,
God planted a garden – a garden of sleep !
'Neath the blue of the sky, in the green of the corn,
It is there that the regal red poppies are born !
Brief days of desire, and long dreams of delight,
They are mine when my poppy land cometh in sight,
Oh ! heart of my heart ! where the poppies are born,
I am waiting for thee, in the hush of the corn.

In my garden of sleep, where the red poppies are spread,
I wait for the living, alone with the dead !
Where a tower in ruins stood guard o'er the deep,
At whose feet were green graves of dear women asleep !
Did they love as I love, when they lived by the sea ?
Did they wait as I wait for the days that may be ?
Oh ! life of my life, on the cliffs by the sea,
By the graves in the grass, I am waiting for thee.

CLEMENT SCOTT.

154

Yarmouth Beach, August Bank Holiday, 1909.

155

The tranquillity of the Broads, 1913-1920.

Yarmouth, of course, had already become a seaside resort. For many years, in common with Lowestoft, it had enjoyed its high reputation at the centre of the herring fishing industry, and it was already well on the way to becoming also the seaside resort of the masses. Again, the great attractions were simply the beach and the sea, and the summer holiday season would find those long stretches of sand almost completely covered by a tightly-packed mass of humanity. There they would sit, their bodies almost completely covered by the dark, heavy clothing of the period – the sun may not have reached their bodies, but at least they could breathe the fresh seaside air. Long rows of deck chairs stood in well-marshalled rows; bathing machines were in place along the shore-line for the hardy bathers; and converted yawls stood ready to take all comers for a trip on the briny. In recent times a change seems to have come over the scene, for the beach never attracts such masses of visitors. Perhaps they prefer the more sophisticated attractions of the Golden Mile, or is it that the old style of family holiday has gone out of favour?

Change, of course, has overtaken us all, and the visitor of today sees a different scene from that of our childhood days. I think Broadland has probably seen the most dramatic transformation, not so much in physical terms as in the type of vessels which now travel along its waterways. The yacht, the rowing boat and the punt are still there, as well as a few lovingly-restored wherries, but the overall picture is now one of vast numbers of motorised launches, not always with experienced sailors at the helm. What, I wonder, is the future for the Broads? Will it become the victim of its own popularity? Of one thing we can be certain – the peace and quiet of those untamed waterways as they were in the early years of this century can now only be found in the memory.

Norfolk has, of course, long been a mecca for painters and writers but, as with other visitors, most of them seem to head for the known areas of natural beauty and miss much of what our county really is like. Our northern coastline between, say, Sheringham and the Wash must surely be one of the finest stretches of land one could ever wish to see, yet I would hesitate to describe it as being typical of the rest of the county. We enjoy such a variety of landscapes that nothing, indeed, could be typical! One man who, I suspect, never visited that coastline must surely have been Noel Coward – how, otherwise, could he have put into the mouth of one of his characters that phrase, "Very flat, Norfolk"?

But a man who fell under the spell of that coastline was Sir Arthur Bryant, the distinguished historian, who, though a Norfolk man by birth, always regarded himself more as a visitor than a native. Because of his father's occupation he was born in 'the little woodland village of Dersingham', on the shores of the Wash. He was, therefore, he said, by birth though in nothing else a Norfolk man. Yet, though he spent only a tiny fraction of his days in the county of his birth and knew at least a dozen English counties better, something within him responded to the nature of his birthplace: "Whenever chance brings me to the coastline where the Sandringham woods keep their wedding with the grey North Sea, the years drop away and I am back where I began".

The nature of his writings clearly gives the lie to his claim to be merely a visitor. He was, without doubt, a man of Norfolk with a Norfolk man's pride in his home county.

It goes without saying, of course, that the city of Norwich has always acted like a magnet to visitors. This is certainly no surprise to those of us who love the place, for we know there is no other city with more to offer to folk who pay it a call. Visitors have come by road, rail and river – and, since 1927, by air, for it was in that year that the Norfolk and Norwich Aero Club was formed, with its aerodrome at Mousehold.

Members of the Royal Family were quick to make use of the new facilities, and it is perhaps not surprising that the Prince of Wales was the first royal visitor. It was on May 30th, 1928 when, after opening Eaton Park, he drove to the aerodrome to witness a flying display arranged in his honour by the Aero Club. At the close of the display he took off in an R.A.F. Bristol fighter, piloted by Flight Lieutenant Don, for his journey home. The royal departure was watched by thousands of delighted citizens, who cheered lustily as the Prince waved from the rising plane.

Prince George flew in on no fewer than three occasions, once arriving quite informally on his way to pay a private visit in the county and then, on June 7th, 1930, to attend the Boy Scout Jamboree at Salhouse. His third visit was in May 1932 when he attended the consecration of the War Memorial Chapel in the Cathedral. His arrival took place in pouring rain; indeed, the weather was so bad that many doubted whether he would come. It was said that the clouds were far too thick and low for flying, but this did not deter His Royal Highness. He arrived in a small cabin aeroplane looking a great deal more comfortable and

The Prince of Wales inspecting aircraft at Mousehold, May 30th, 1928.

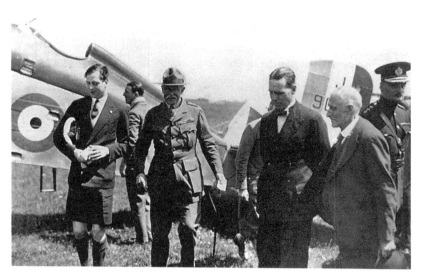

Prince George arriving at Mousehold for the Boy Scout Jamboree at Salhouse,
June 7th, 1930.

cheerful than the many spectators huddling beneath dripping umbrellas.

On June 21st, 1933, the Prince of Wales was back again for probably the greatest occasion of them all. The Club aerodrome had been extended, levelled and re-turfed and he was to open it as the city's first Municipal Aerodrome. He arrived at 11-45 a.m. to be greeted by a distinguished body of civic dignitaries and a large crowd of spectators. After declaring the Aerodrome open, he inspected the new premises and also a flight of Sidestrand aircraft from No.101 (Bomber) Squadron of the Royal Air Force. Then, at 12-15 p.m., he took off to fly to the Royal Norfolk Agricultural Show at King's Lynn, after which the assembled crowds were entertained by a flying display by the Sidestrand aircraft.

One final visitor is worthy of mention, and he came more conventionally by road rather than by air. He was J.B. Priestley and it was Norwich rather than the county that attracted him, for he was a city man and, furthermore, he was eager to meet once again his great friend R.H. Mottram. For a Yorkshireman, I feel he summed us up rather well:

"The East Anglian," he said, "is a solid man. Lots of beef and beer, tempered with east wind, have gone to the making of him. Once he is sure you are not going to cheat him or be very grand and affected, he is a friendly chap; but if you want the other thing you can have it".

And his views on Norwich? I think they provide a fitting conclusion to this review of Norfolk visitors.

"What a grand, higgledy-piggledy, sensible old place Norwich is," he said. And he left the city with one last wish – that he might live to see the Senators of the Eastern Province, stout men who take mustard with their beef and beer with their mustard (his words, not mine!) march through Tombland to assemble in their capital.

CHAPTER 18

Gipsy Smith – Evangelist.

Cornelius Smith and Mary Welch were gipsies – it was pure Romany blood that coursed through their veins. They had become man and wife according to Romany lore around 1850, though such a union was not recognised by the Established Church. This fact, however, was of no great concern to them, for most gipsies at that time cared little for religion and knew almost nothing of God.

Strangely enough, they always took steps to get their babies christened, and there were two reasons for this. Firstly, it just seemed the right thing to do, and then there was the fact that it was a matter of business. The clergyman of the nearest parish church was invited to come to the encampment and perform the ceremony. To the 'gorgios' (people who are not gipsies) the event was one of rare and curious interest. Some of the ladies of the congregation were sure to accompany the parson to see the gipsy baby, and it was unlikely that they would do so without bringing presents for the gipsy mother and, more often, the baby.

Cornelius and Mary (usually known as Polly) travelled widely throughout the eastern counties – Norfolk, Suffolk, Essex, Bedfordshire and Hertfordshire, with their winter quarters in Cambridge. They scraped a living by selling the wooden clothes pegs that Cornelius made, and from the occasional tinkering jobs that came his way. Apart from an occasional few days in Cambridge, their six children had no schooling, but what they lacked in book learning they more than made up for in their knowledge of the natural world of the countryside. They were a simple, ordinary gipsy family, yet one of those children was destined to become arguably the greatest evangelist the world had seen, with his name a household word throughout five continents.

That child was their fourth, a little boy whom they named Rodney. They had set up their tent in the shade of an old hornbeam tree in Epping Forest, and it was there, on March 31st, 1860, that Rodney made his entry into the world. Ahead of him lay 87 years of sorrow and joy, heartbreak and delight – a life of such dedication as is the lot of only a privileged few.

Rodney was to encounter much tragedy in his long life, and the first – and undoubtedly the greatest – came upon him when he was just a small boy, little more than six years old. The family were travelling in Hertfordshire when the oldest child, a girl, was taken ill. The nearest town was Baldock, and Cornelius immediately made haste in that direction so that he might get a doctor for his stricken daughter. Once there, the doctor came out and, mounting the steps of the caravan, leaned over the door and called the sick child to him.

"Your child has the smallpox," announced the doctor. "You must get out of the town at once".

He directed them to a country lane about a mile and a half away – it was called Norton Lane. In a little bend of the lane, on the left-hand side, between a huge overhanging hawthorn and some trees, making a natural arch, Cornelius erected their tent. There he left Polly and four children. He took the waggon two hundred yards further down the lane and stood it on the right-hand side near an old chalkpit. From the door he could see the tent clearly and be within call. The waggon was the sick-room and Cornelius was the nurse.

A few days later the doctor, coming to the tent, discovered that one of the boys, Ezekiel, also had smallpox, and he too was sent to the waggon, so that Cornelius now had two invalids to nurse. Poor Polly would wander up and down the lane in a state of great agitation, crying again and again, "My poor children will die, and I am not allowed to go to them". She had to go into Baldock to buy food and, after preparing it in the tent, would carry it half-way from there to the waggon. Then she would put it on the ground and attract Cornelius' attention so that he could come and collect it. But each day Polly, in the anxiety of her loving heart, got a little nearer to the waggon until, one day, she went too near, and then she also became ill. When the doctor made his next call he diagnosed it as smallpox.

Cornelius was in the utmost distress. His worst fears were realised. He had been determined to save Polly, for he loved her as only a gipsy can love. She was the wife of his youth and the mother of his children. They were both very young when they married, not much over twenty, and they were still quite young. He would have died to save her. He had kept the two halves of his family apart for a whole month to avoid infection, but now she, too, was smitten. He felt that all hope had gone, and he brought the waggon back to the tent. There lay mother and sister and brother, all three struck low with smallpox. Then, a few days later, a little baby was born.

Polly's condition soon became worse until she, herself, knew she was dying. Cornelius' hands were stretched out to hold her, but they were not strong enough. Other hands, omnipotent and eternal, were taking her from him. He sat by her and told her all he knew of the Gospel, at which she threw her arms around his neck and kissed him. Then he went outside, stood behind the waggon and wept. When he went back inside, she looked calmly into his face and said, "I want you to promise me one thing. Will you be a good father to my children?" He promised her that he would; at that moment he would have promised her anything. Again he went outside and, as tears once more began to flow, he heard her singing something he had never heard before:

"I have a Father in the promised land;
My God calls me, I must go
To meet Him in the promised land".

Again Cornelius went back into the caravan.

"Polly, my dear," he said, "where did you learn that song?"

"I heard it when I was a little girl," said Polly. "One Sunday my father's tents were pitched on a village green and, seeing the young people and others going into a little chapel, I followed them in and they sang those words".

It must have been at least twenty years since Polly had heard those lines, but they came back to her as she sought the salvation of the God she had never known.

"I'm not afraid to die now," she said. "I feel that everything will be alright. I feel sure that God will take care of my children".

Cornelius watched over her all that Sunday night and knew that she was sinking fast. When Monday morning dawned it found her deep in prayer.

Rodney wandered up the lane that morning hand-in-hand with his sister Tilly. The two little things were inseparable, and they could not go to their father, for he was too full of his own grief. Then, suddenly, he heard his name being called and, turning back, he met his sister Emily.

"Rodney," she said. "Mother's dead".

The news hit him with the force of a thunderbolt. He fell flat on his face as though he had been shot, and he lay there, weeping his heart out.

An indescribable gloom settled down upon the little encampment in Norton Lane, and then came the day of the funeral. Polly was to be buried at the dead of night, for the authorities would not permit the funeral to take place in the daytime. As darkness fell, along came an old farm cart. Polly's coffin was placed in the vehicle and, between ten and eleven o'clock, Cornelius, the only mourner, followed her to the grave by lantern light. There she was laid to rest in Norton churchyard.

A fortnight later the little baby died and was placed at her mother's side. Polly and her last-born lie in that portion of the graveyard where are interred the remains of the poor, the unknown and the forsaken. A few weeks later, all danger of infection being over, the doctor gave the rest of the family leave to move from the lane where they had seen so much sorrow.

The scene in Norton Lane on the morning that Polly died was to remain for ever etched into young Rodney's mind. He was only a little fellow but, even in his later years, he could close his eyes and see the gipsy tent and waggon in the lane. There was the fire burning outside on the ground, the kettle hanging over it in true gipsy fashion, and a bucket of water nearby. Some clothes that his father had been washing hung on the hedge, and the old horse was grazing along the lane. He could visualise the boughs bending in the breeze and he could almost hear the singing of the birds. But there was one thing that had forever faded from his memory – and it was the most precious of all.

"When I try to call back the appearance of my dear mother," he said, "I am baffled. That dear face that bent over my cradle and sang lullabies to me; that mother who, if she had lived, would have been more to me than any other in God's world – her face has faded clean from my memory".

Not surprisingly, Polly's death had a profound effect on her family, not least her grieving husband. Cornelius went through the days like a soul in torment, a ship without a rudder. He had the strongest urge to find God but had not the slightest idea as to how he could achieve that ambition. His talent as a fiddler, indeed, became a handicap for, playing as he did in public houses all over the region, he found it difficult to resist the temptation to partake too freely of the drink that he was offered. As the years went by, he would take Rodney with him to dance to jigs and to go round with the collecting cap when the effect of the alcohol began to have a disastrous effect on his playing.

The grave of Gipsy Smith's mother and baby sister,
Norton Churchyard, near Baldock, Herts.

Then, when all seemed lost, he finally decided to seek conversion to Christianity. It was in Shepherd's Bush – when there were still some green fields in that London suburb – that he vowed not to move until his search for God had ended. To indicate his sincerity, he sold his horse, an action never taken lightly by a gipsy. Then he had a chance meeting with an old roadmender, who told him that there was to be a meeting that very night at the Latimer Road Mission Hall.

"You come with me to that meeting and you'll be alright," said the roadmender.

Cornelius went, was converted and declared his faith. When he came home after the meeting, he gathered his family around him.

"Children," he said, "God has made a new man of me. You have a new father".

His conversion affected all the family, most of all Rodney, who had by then entered his teens and felt the urge to follow his father. He had heard of John Bunyan, who had been something of a sinner but had been converted and had then produced a great written work for God. Quite by chance, their next stopping place was near Bedford – Bunyan's home town. There, as he stood at the foot of the statue of John Bunyan, he decided he would live for God and go on to meet his mother in Heaven.

A few days later the family moved to Cambridge, and it was there that Rodney publicly committed himself to God. He went to a meeting at the small Primitive Methodist Chapel in Fitzroy Street, and there, during the singing of a Gospel hymn, he went forward and knelt at the communion rail. As he knelt, he heard somebody whisper, "Oh, it's only a gipsy boy". But the minister spoke to him: "Do you know what you are doing? It is a great step to take, giving one's life to Jesus".

"Well," said Rodney, "I can't trust myself, for I am nothing; I can't trust in what I have, for I have nothing; and I can't trust in what I know, for I know nothing. It won't be hard for me to trust Jesus".

He was then sixteen and knew more of the ways of Nature than many would learn in a lifetime, but he now sought book learning, and he acquired three large books – the Bible, an English Dictionary and a Bible Dictionary. He carried them everywhere, much to the amusement of his family.

"Never you mind," he said. "One day I'll be able to read them. And," he added, "I'm going to preach too".

That was on November 17th, 1876, and from then on he took every chance to improve himself. He asked questions and, as he went about the country lanes selling his father's clothes pegs, he practiced his preaching. One day he entered a turnip field and preached most eloquently to the turnips. In later years he often told this story in his sermons: "Not one of them made an attempt to move away".

Just one year later came his first address to a public meeting. It was a meeting of the Christian Mission at their headquarters in Whitechapel Road in East London, and it was presided over by the Rev. William Booth. He went purely as a member of the congregation, hence his state of shock when, after several speakers had addressed the meeting, the Rev. Mr. Booth announced: "The next speaker will be the gipsy boy". Rodney's first inclination, he later admitted, was to run away, but he started with a religious song and then spoke of his humble beginnings and how Jesus had saved him. After the meeting, William Booth asked him to give up his home life and join the Christian Mission. Rodney agreed, and that day, June 25th, 1877, marked the beginning of a career that was to inspire millions of people in five continents.

In the years that followed, he travelled widely over Britain, staying at each place for as long as it took him to lay down foundations on which others could build. There was Sheffield, Whitby – where he was to meet his future wife – and Bolton, where he had to contend with riots and physical abuse. Then, in 1879, the Christian Mission became the Salvation Army and the gipsy boy became Lieutenant Rodney Smith. He was sent to Plymouth, where he became Captain Smith, and then on to Chatham, where the soldiers and sailors took great delight in disrupting his meetings. Then it was Hull, where as many as fifteen hundred converts would gather for prayer meetings at 7 o'clock on Sunday mornings, and where they sold 15,000 copies of *The War Cry* every week. His work at Derby was less successful, but then, in 1882, came his greatest triumph. It was at Hanley where, after twelve months of tremendous success, the leaders of the Free Churches of the town decided to show their appreciation by raising money to present him with a gold watch. It bore the inscription: "Presented to Gipsy Rodney Smith as a memento of high esteem and in recognition of his valuable services in Hanley and district, July 1882". His wife and his sister Tilly each received a gift of five pounds.

168

Gipsy Smith in middle age.

Then, a fortnight later, came a day which he was never to forget. It began with great joy but finished with utter despair. The joy was occasioned by the arrival of his second child, a boy whom he named Hanley in recognition of the town where he had achieved such success and found such happiness. Then, just two hours later, he received a letter from Bramwell Booth. It read:

We understand that on Monday, July 31st, a presentation of a gold watch was made to you at Hanley, accompanied by a purse containing £5 to your wife, and the same to your sister. We can only conclude that this has been done in premeditated defiance of the rules and regulations of the Army to which you have repeatedly given your adherence, and that you have fully resolved no longer to continue with us. It is clear that neither you nor your sister can work in the Army any longer as officers, and the General directs me to say that we have arranged for the appointment of officers to succeed you at Hanley at once.

Gipsy was greatly shocked and hurt, but I have a suspicion that he left the Salvation Army with mixed feelings. He found the manner of his dismissal curt and hurtful, but he had never really enjoyed the Army's discipline, and now his free spirit could work in other ways. Henceforth, he could go wherever he was asked.

This he did, to even greater effect, and in January 1889 he set sail for America, where he was destined to become just as famous and well-loved as in England. Many other trips across the Atlantic followed, his arrival on each occasion being greeted with brass bands and flying flags, and then he spread his wings to South Africa and Australia.

All the while, he and his brother Ezekiel continued their ministry in this country, and Norfolk was not forgotten. In 1912 he preached at the Surrey Chapel in Norwich; in 1916 he visited the Methodist Church in Lady Lane, where the crush of people to hear him was so great that two people suffered broken legs, and children were passed over the heads of the crowd to places of safety. In 1921 Ezekiel held a 10-day mission in the Methodist Chapel at Forncett St. Peter; just before Easter, 1927, he preached in the Baptist Chapel at Old Buckenham; and later he attended a mission in the Gospel Hut at Tibenham.

Then, on July 2nd, 1938, at the age of 78, Gipsy Smith dropped a bombshell on the world by marrying for a second time. He had lost his first wife some years earlier, and the mere fact of his

Gipsy Smith leaving on one of his trips to the U.S.A.

taking to himself a new bride was not in itself too surprising. It was his choice of partner, however, which caused a few raised eyebrows, for she was no less than fifty years younger than himself – a mere 28! But it was the best thing he could have done, for no woman of his age could have kept up with him, and she herself was a remarkable woman. Mary Alice Shaw was a University graduate in English Literature – and a warm-hearted Christian.

They spent the years of the Second World War in America, travelling all over that continent, and all the time his young wife was by his side. At the end of the War they returned to England, but Rodney was now old and physically weak. They lived in a flat in London, but he felt restless and imprisoned. He went to Epping Forest to visit the hornbeam tree under whose branches he had been born. He remained lively, but his voice and his heart were failing. The only solution, said his friends, was another trip to America for a season in the Florida sunshine.

So it was that, in the summer of 1947, Mary Alice and Gipsy Smith boarded the *Queen Mary* on her first post-war trip to America. The band was playing and the flags were flying when, on August 4th, the liner reached her destination – but they were

171

Gipsy Smith addressing a congregation in Epping Forest.

not in celebration of Rodney's arrival. He had already completed his life's journey – he had died on board the liner.

Now, in a grassy spot known as Mill Plain in Epping Forest, against the hornbeam tree under which he was born, a carved block of Cornish granite marks his memory. It bears the inscription:

Gipsy Rodney Smith, M.B.E.,
who preached the Gospel to thousands on five continents
for seventy years, was born here March 31st, 1860, and
called home, journeying to America, August 4th, 1947.

CHAPTER 19

Ally Sloper – Rebel.

It is, perhaps, stretching things slightly to include a fictional character amongst earlier visitors to Norfolk, but Ally Sloper played such a notable part in the lives of our grandparents that such inclusion seems justified.

Ally Sloper was the brainchild of a London writer, Gilbert Dalziel, who brought him into the world to cheer up the populace during the economic recession of the 1880s. Every Saturday, at the cost of one penny, his latest activities, together with his comments on matters of the day, were chronicled in *Ally Sloper's Half Holiday,* which can well claim to have been the first weekly comic paper.

Ally Sloper was a somewhat grotesque figure of a man, ungainly in build and endowed with an almost-bald head and the most bulbous of noses. These attributes, together with his shabby frock coat and battered top hat made him strangely reminiscent of that great American comedy actor, W.C. Fields; but it was his attitude to authority which most endeared him to the public, for he was undoubtedly the Angry Young Man of his day.

At first glance the publication seemed modest enough, but the comments which Gilbert Dalziel attributed to his anti-hero were richly barbed with ill-concealed attempts at deflating the famous and the pompous. There were, for instance, frequent references to "Mr. Frunt-Paige, the Editor of *The Daily Sellegraph"*. There was much comment concerning clerical gentlemen, one of whom was portrayed in a cartoon asking a lady parishioner for her reaction to the cushions which had been provided on the pews in his church.

"Quite splendid," replied the lady. "Such a great aid towards peaceful sleep during long and boring sermons".

Nor was Mr. Sloper's lampoonery confined only to personalities. Week by week his journal carried advertisements which were direct parodies of those for real products. So skilfully were they designed that readers had great difficulty in deciding whether the goods were real or bogus. There was the advertisement for "Sloper's Pills", which had the appearance of being completely

Ally Sloper's Half Holiday

FOUNDED AND CONDUCTED BY GILBERT DALZIEL

Vol. XIV.—No. 708.　　SATURDAY, NOVEMBER 20, 1897.　　ONE PENNY.

THE DEMON BILL-POSTER.

"I can fully appreciate Poor Papa's anxiety to obtain the widest publicity for his 'Christmas Holidays,' to be published on December 6th, but there is a limit even to sensational advertising. From personal inspection, I know that Dad's annual Twopenn'orth will be the 'greatest thing he's ever done; but when it comes to placarding Nelson's Column and the Trafalgar Square lions—why, it's 'time to draw the line. Papa says his enthusiasm over his marvellous production got the better of his judgment, and luckily for him and Alec the authorities saw it in the same light, or there would have been trouble."—TOOTSIE.

A copy of Ally Sloper's weekly comic paper published in November, 1897.

genuine. For the sum of 9½d one could obtain a box of 50 pills, guaranteed to provide relief from all stomach ailments, liver complaints and headache. One can only wonder how many readers sent their 9½d for this cure-all remedy.

On another occasion he announced the forthcoming meeting of the directors of "The United General Whelk Supply Association", an organisation with himself as Chairman and capital of £5,000,000. Readers were invited to write for details to the Secretary (A. Sloper Esq.) or to send money in stamps direct to the Treasurer (also himself).

174

New inventions were also a regular feature of *Ally Sloper's Half Holiday*. One of the most ingenious was a contraption called the "Piano-Fiend Pulveriser", which was a rotating wheel of gloved artificial hands which, when set in motion, would thump a piano keyboard and produce a very loud, and equally discordant, cacophony of sound. It was designed, readers were told, to counteract the heartbreak which music lovers must have felt when they heard the next-door neighbours' child murdering good music during piano practice. The idea was that, once wound up and set in motion, the contraption would continue working for eight hours, during which time the owner could pop out for an evening at the Music Hall!

Though obviously the main player in Mr. Dalziel's charade, Ally Sloper was by no means the only character in his weekly paper. There was, for instance, his young assistant, Alec, who helped his master with such tasks as bill-posting in Trafalgar Square; there was Tommy Truffles, who might well lay claim to being one of the earliest of comic strip heroes; and there was Ally Sloper's equally fictitious daughter, Tootsie, who brought an air of femininity to the scene with her fashion news for the ladies. Best-loved of all, however, were the Rumfoozlers – a group of men "diligently devoted to the concept of having a good time". Their activities always seemed to involve the consumption of large quantities of alcohol, which was not always helpful on such occasions as, for instance, when they went looking for Halley's Comet!

But the unchallenged star of the weekly was Ally Sloper. He was a bibulous rebel with no respect for the Establishment. He was a total resister of change, preferring to lead his life to his own satisfaction. He was irreverent and uncouth, with no time for social graces or anything resembling gentility. Perhaps that is why his readers looked upon him with such reverence, for, even a century ago, people had a soft spot for a rebel. Perhaps that is why, also, people masquerading as Ally Sloper were always to be seen at Fancy Dress events like that Ice Carnival on Diss Mere in January 1891.

The weekly paper was a tremendous success and is said to have made a fortune, a penny at a time, for its creator. It survived the death of its original illustrator, William Giles Baxter, in 1888, and continued well into the present century with drawings by W.F. Thomas. It claimed the largest circulation of any illustrated paper in the world and, at the turn of the century, could be sent post free to any part of the globe (except Sarawak and Bechuanaland) for 6s 6d per year. I fear we shall never know why those two countries were excluded.

At one stage Ally Sloper offered his Award of Merit, entitling the holder to become a Fellow of the Order of Slopery, to people who achieved success in their own particular walk of life. I was once proudly told by an acquaintance that his father was one of only two persons to win the award, but I had not the heart to tell him that I knew of at least a dozen in this county alone, ranging from skill at quoits to proficiency on the flute and piccolo. The only surviving example I have seen, still greatly cherished by the owner's descendants, reads:

This is to Certify That
THE SLOPER AWARD OF MERIT
has been granted to GUNNER T. PHILLIPS

Because he won the 1st Prize for Carbine Shooting in No.1 Battery. And be it understood that from this date henceforth and in all or any circumstances whatever, wherever and whatwithstanding, he shall be entitled to affix to his name in any manner, however absurdly underlined or offensively conspicuous, the mystic letters F.O.S.

But it is further directed that anyone suspected of adopting the same under false and fraudulent pretence be thereon and thereby, notwithstanding, rigorously searched, rattled up and rummaged generally and elsewhere and told they ought not to in a severe tone of voice. This is final.

GIVEN UNDER MY HAND AND SEAL
This twenty-second day of December, 1892
(Signed) Ally Sloper.

While *Ally Sloper's Half Holiday* brought fame to Mr. Sloper and success to Gilbert Dalziel, it also brought inspiration to a young aspiring publisher named Alfred Harmsworth. He decided that there was a market for a new weekly comic paper and, in 1890, he introduced *Comic Cuts,* which was to blossom for sixty years and bring pleasure to many of us in our childhood days. As the years went by, there followed *Chips* and *Funny Wonder* – and young Alfred grew up to become Lord Northcliffe, the creator of the *Daily Mail.* But that, as they say, is another story.

CHAPTER 20

Amy, Wonderful Amy.

Looking back to the years of my boyhood, I get the distinct impression that there was never the amount of news that nowadays assails our eardrums – or is my memory playing tricks?

Admittedly, we had no television to invade our living room with its uncomfortable sense of urgency; the newsreader on the wireless presented his tidings with a marked degree of decorum; and our newspapers were merely a slimline foretaste of the multi-paged productions of today. But I cannot put full trust in my boyhood memory. I feel sure that momentous events were taking place all over the world, yet my brain was very selective – it only chose to register those happenings which were of interest to a young boy.

Take, for example, 1930 – a truly splendid year. It was the year when a young Australian cricketer named Don Bradman scored 334 runs in an innings at Lord's. The fact that, in the previous year, he had made a world's record score of 452 not out merely increased his stature in our eyes, and our only regret was that he was not an Englishman. That year, also, Cambridge won the Boat Race for the seventh successive time, much to my disgust but to the delight of my brother Peter. He and I never supported the same team in any sporting event – in football his choice was Arsenal, while I plumped for a rather obscure Scottish team known as Hamilton Academicals. Success rarely came their way, but I liked the sound of their name!

It was the year when a great new ship, the *Empress of Britain,* was launched by the Prince of Wales, and when Britain's largest motor vessel, the White Star liner *Britannic,* sailed from Liverpool to New York on her maiden voyage. The airship R100 reached 81$\frac{1}{2}$ miles an hour in a trial flight and later, having sailed from Cardington to Montreal in 79 hours, completed the return trip in 57 hours.

But there was tragedy too. The R101 struck a hillside and burst into flames in France, with only six out of a total of 54 passengers and crew surviving. Sir Henry Segrave was fatally injured on Lake

Amy Johnson in the cabin of her Puss Moth.

Windermere after having achieved a new water speed record in *Miss England II.*

But, of all the events of 1930, there was one which still stands out in glorious memory – it was the year when Amy Johnson made her solo flight from England to Australia. Leaving Croydon on May 5th, the journey took her almost three weeks, reaching Port Darwin on May 24th and then being greeted in Sydney by a huge, cheering crowd. The fact that this mere slip of a woman could succeed in such a perilous venture seemed incredible and, while the world applauded, the people of Britain took Amy to their hearts. Somebody even wrote a song about her – "Amy, Wonderful Amy". She hated it and visibly cringed whenever she heard it, but the public seized upon it and sang it with gusto.

Ten months after her flight, the people of Norwich had their chance to show their affection when Amy visited the City. It was on March 17th, 1931, and she was to be guest of honour and principal speaker at the Norfolk and Norwich Aero Club's Annual Ball at the Spring Gardens.

Not surprisingly, her mode of transport from London was her yellow Puss Moth aeroplane, *Jason II,* and, long before her arrival, a large crowd began to gather on Mousehold Aerodrome, where the Club had its headquarters. In due course, a statement was made

178

that Miss Johnson had left London at 3-30 p.m., but she was not expected to arrive until 5 o'clock as she was flying into a strong head wind all the way. From time to time, the crowd's patient wait was enlivened by other planes flying in, but none of them proved to be Amy, nor even Colonel Shelmerdine, the Director of Civil Aviation, who was expected at about the same time. Eventually, just after 5 o'clock, two aeroplanes were seen approaching the aerodrome from the south-west. They carried out the traditional manoeuvre of making a graceful circle of the aerodrome before landing within a few seconds of each other and taxiing together across to the hangars.

A rousing cheer went up as Amy Johnson was recognised. Colonel Shelmerdine and his wife alighted from the other machine and were welcomed by Captain Harmer, Chairman of the Club, and other officials, while Amy was received by her hosts, Mr. and Mrs. Tim Green (of the well-known outfitting store) and their young daughter, Pat. The original plan had been to give one of the past Chairmen the honour of accommodating Amy for the night but, in view of the fact that he was a bachelor, it was thought more suitable for her to stay the night with the Green family at their Earlham Road home. After exchanging the traditional pleasantries and posing for photographs, the party were led into the Clubhouse for tea by young Pat who, in a great state of excitement, was heard to express her regret that Miss Johnson was only staying for one night. "I shan't have time to ask her half the things I want to," she said.

Later that evening, upwards of 240 people sat down for dinner at the now long-departed Spring Gardens in Mountergate. The music was to be provided by the Spring Gardens Band under the direction of that doyen of the local music scene, Percy Cohen, and the top table had something of the look of a partial Who's-Who of the county's worthies. Apart from Captain and Mrs. Harmer, those present included the Lord Lieutenant of Norfolk (Mr. Russell J. Colman), the Lord Mayor of Norwich (Miss Mabel Clarkson), Mr. H.N. Holmes (President of the Club) and Mrs. Holmes, the Chief Constable of Norfolk (Captain S.H. Van Neck), Mr. Archie Rice, Mr. Bullough (City Engineer), Mr. Cecil Gowing (Vice Chairman of the Club), and Mr. C. Watling (ex-Sheriff of Norwich) and Mrs. Watling.

The speeches that followed the dinner gave a clear insight into the feelings of the various speakers concerning a topic which was

Amy Johnson is welcomed at Mousehold, March 17th, 1931.

Little Pat Green leads her parents and Amy Johnson
into the clubhouse for tea.

under discussion at the time – the possible building of a municipal aerodrome. They also painted a clear picture of flying as it was in the thirties, which makes Amy Johnson's flight all the more remarkable.

First on his feet was Russell Colman, Lord Lieutenant and the county's most popular after-dinner speaker with a fund of Norfolk stories to suit every occasion. Proposing the toast of "Civil Aviation", he said that he had no intention of making a speech on the subject, except to chaff aviators about the noise they made when flying.

"If I tried to make the same noise on the ground with a motor car," he said, "my friend the Chief Constable of Norfolk would soon be on my track". (Laughter).

He admitted that he had never been up in the air (Cries of 'Shame!') and he was afraid he never felt any desire to do so. He confessed to a much greater liking for sea travel – even when the sea was rough – and this brought him conveniently to the first of a succession of his stories. It concerned a very stormy sea crossing from Norway to England during which the hundred or so passengers were so badly affected by the pitching and tossing of the ship that only half a dozen of their number were physically capable of assembling for dinner. The parson rose and said Grace: "For what we are about to retain may the Lord make us truly thankful".

More stories followed, to the great enjoyment of the assembled company, and he concluded by repeating that he had never been up in the air. "But," he said to tremendous applause, "I have had the honour of shaking hands with Miss Amy Johnson".

Mabel Clarkson was the next speaker, and she soon nailed her colours to the mast as regards the proposed municipal aerodrome.

"I had better admit," she said, "that my own particular interest in it is from the unemployment point of view. It is an ideal unemployment scheme, for the levelling can practically all be done by unemployed labour. But I'm afraid that argument alone will not persuade the Council to embark on what is, of course, a very costly undertaking".

She was glad to hear that the Aero Club did not propose to have a big air display that year, because she had been told that the chief attraction to the general public in a flying meeting was probably the novelty and the element of danger.

"I think," she said, "there is no meaner crowd characteristic than that of watching other people endanger their lives purely for the pleasure and amusement of that same crowd, half of whom wouldn't go up in an aeroplane if they had the chance".

Then it was Amy Johnson's turn and, after the hearty cheer that greeted her had subsided, she said that she had no greater pleasure than meeting people connected with, and interested in, aviation. She had never before been to Norwich, but having sampled the excellence of the Aerodrome, she was sure of coming again.

"Every city worthy of the name of city," she said, "will have to have an aerodrome sooner or later, and the people who will get the chief glory are those who have the courage and devotion now to get on with the job instead of waiting until every other city has got an aerodrome. Norwich ought not to be content with being passed by on the way from London to the North. It should be at once a calling place, and then everyone who had come once and found it a place of wonderful hospitality would want to come again".

"The Lord Lieutenant," she continued, "had one grouse to make against us aviators; he says that we make too much noise. I think we have got to make some noise, otherwise we should not be noticed. We do not like to fly along to an aerodrome and find there only a caretaker who has gone to sleep. In this country, and in Europe generally, not enough attention is paid to guiding aircraft from the ground. There ought to be a certain number of landmarks so that aviators may know where they are. For people using cars on the roads you put up plenty of signs. The poor people up in the air have no help at all except to come down and ask their way. Then trouble arises, especially if in coming down we trample a field of corn".

The assembled company listened intently but, as she came to the end of her speech, there must surely have been one thought uppermost in their minds – how on Earth did Amy Johnson find her way to Australia?

CHAPTER 21

Out With Romany.

For a period of ten years, from 1933 onwards, one of the most welcome of guests regularly found his way into thousands of Norfolk homes for a weekly visit – and he did it without ever setting foot in our fair county. His presence among us was brought about by the miracle of wireless, and he was known simply as "Romany".

Romany was the first great naturalist broadcaster and, with his genial personality, his soothing, dark velvet voice and, above all, his rare genius for communication, he held us all spellbound as he described the natural wonders of the countryside. During those ten years he became the most popular of all children's broadcasters, with a nationwide audience of 13 million listeners.

The programme would begin with the playing of his signature tune – "Lullaby of the Leaves". Then, as the music slowly faded, the announcer's voice would be heard: "And now, children, we are going ... Out With Romany". Then, with his faithful dog Raq, a blue roan cocker spaniel, Romany would wander through the countryside describing the things he saw – birds and animals, country crafts – nothing escaped his eager attention. And there, too, were the sounds of the countryside. When he stood by a stream, his listeners heard the water trickling over the stones; when he lit a fire outside his gipsy caravan, there was the crackling of the sticks; and, as he passed through a gateway from one field to another, the squeaking of the hinges marked his progress. Country folk readily recognised many of the things he described, but to children in the slums of an inner city it must have been a world of fantasy. They may not have known what a skylark looked like, but they soon got to know the sound of its song, for they had heard it when they went out with Romany.

Throughout his ten years of broadcasting, there were two things of which most of his listeners were unaware. Firstly, there was the fact that, despite their apparent authenticity, the programmes were all carried out in a B.B.C. studio. This was a closely-guarded secret until, after Romany's death, the truth was revealed in an article in the *Radio Times*. I have always thought it unfortunate that the illusion should have been shattered in that way, but, anyway, not many of his listeners believed the revelation, for they had been with the man, step by step, as he took them through the countryside.

The other secret was that, though a countryman at heart, his occupation demanded that he should spend much of his time in town and city, for he was an ordained Methodist minister. There was a wealth of gipsy blood coursing through his veins, however, for his mother was Tilly Smith, sister of the renowned Romany evangelist Gipsy Smith. Tilly had married Lieutenant George Evens, a Salvation Army officer from Plymouth and, in 1883, she brought into the world the little boy whom they christened George Bramwell. He travelled around with his parents and, while they were busy with religious matters, he would escape into the surrounding countryside to explore the wonders of nature.

"I do not remember a time," he later wrote, "when the countryside had no fascination for me. Give me a lane and a hedge, and heaven lies in exploring its shadows and becoming intimate with its shy inhabitants. Probably this is due to the fact that I spring from pure gipsy stock. In my veins runs the blood of nomads who have sought the solitudes for a host of centuries. It is this ancestry which has made me a roamer and, like a bird hearing its migratory call, so the fields and the woods lure me from city life".

As a young man, George Bramwell Evens decided to enter the Methodist ministry and, after his ordination in 1908, his first appointment was to Dalston in East London. At first glance, the idea of having to live in such an area must have had little appeal to such a lover of the countryside, but it carried with it two compensations. Firstly, it was not too many miles from Epping Forest, and it was to that Romany heaven that he would escape whenever his ministry duties permitted. Then there was his meeting with Eunice Thomas, a pretty girl from the neighbouring Congregational Church. Romance blossomed and they later married and were blessed with a son, Glyn, and a daughter whom they named Romany June.

At one stage in his early life, for some reason known only to himself, he tried to join the Army, but fortunately he was rejected because of a heart murmur. It was then that he turned to professional writing under the pen-name of "The Tramp". It would seem that this title was highly appropriate for, though he was neatly dressed when attending to his ministry, he was renowned for his scruffy appearance when out on his rambles through the countryside. He was well aware of this reputation and I believe it gave him secret pleasure.

"I ought to say at once," he wrote, "that I am a 'tramp' by choice and not of necessity. Lingering in the city, either to gaze at shop windows or to be amused by some 'show', is not my highest form of bliss. I prefer to loiter in green meadows, to explore the fringes of quiet pools and the margins of laughing streams, to muse under shadowed hedges – in a word, to potter about where the wild birds sing or where the trout rises to the fly".

During the years that followed, his literary output was nothing less than prodigious. For 17 years he contributed a weekly nature column extending to 2,000 words to the *Cumberland News,* and for 23 years he did likewise for the *Methodist Recorder.* The *Yorkshire Post* and the *Huddersfield Examiner* regularly featured his work, as did the *Sunday Circle,* a popular Christian weekly publication of that time.

Then, in 1933, somebody suggested that he ought to consider auditioning for the B.B.C. They welcomed him with open arms as a splendid addition to the staff of Children's Hour, but there was one small problem – what could they call him? Most of the contributors to that programme were known as 'Uncle This' or 'Auntie That', but Bramwell had no wish to be addressed in that manner. Nor did he favour 'The Reverend Evens'.

"I know!" he said. "Just call me 'Romany' ".

So it was that this remarkable character was launched upon his biggest-ever audience who, in their millions, readily succumbed to the compelling delight of his tramps through the countryside. He continued his writing and also his talks for children, which gave him great delight. He always took Raq with him on these occasions, but the faithful cocker was kept in the wings when his master started speaking. Then, at a suitable moment, Romany would ask his young listeners: "Would you like to see Raq?"

"Yes, please!" would come the full-throated cry from the children.

Then, to their utter delight, Raq would come bounding on to the stage and, with one great leap, would land in Romany's arms. It was a moment of sheer joy, for they had heard the dog barking on the wireless and now they were really seeing him!

Romany.

Raq.

All the while, he continued his writing, and a long succession of books was avidly seized upon by his adoring admirers. Each one would be sold out within a very short time of its appearance in the shops, and his number of reprints must have been the envy of many of his fellow-writers. Among the nine which still occupy a prized place on my shelves there is one much-revered First Edition and another bearing the imprint "Sixteenth Impression, June 1947" – eighteen years after its original publication!

His books were, of course, mainly directed at the younger generation, though he numbered many an adult among his followers. Furthermore, he wrote in a manner which typified his natural modesty, for he cast himself as the visitor from the town learning the ways of the countryside from the people who lived there. Thus we met John Fell the gamekeeper, Jerry the poacher and Ned, the village postman. There, too, were Alan and Joe – both farmers – John Rubb, the angler, and that delightful character Sally Stordy. Sally was a cottager who regularly took her eggs to sell at the nearby market, and it was there that Romany had his first lesson in the way rural business transactions were carried out.

He had gone to the market and found Sally standing behind a well-scrubbed table on which she was displaying her wares. They spoke for a while and then she left him and moved away to speak to a friend. It was at that moment that a hard-featured woman came up and, after a fleeting glance at Romany, bent her head over the eggs in Sally's basket as though she was judging them by the smell.

"What are the eggs?" she rapped out like a drill sergeant.

Romany was rather taken aback by this onslaught, for never before had he been mistaken for a purveyor of farmyard commodities. However, he rose to the occasion and, after swallowing hard, he replied professionally:

"These," he said, pointing to the brown ones, "are laid by Rhode Island Reds, whilst these (pointing to the white ones) are produced by White Leg--".

"No," said the customer with a scornful note. "How much are you asking?"

"One and five a dozen," he replied.

"Ye'll have to come down a bit, I reckon," she replied – and off she went.

Romany watched her as she went on her way, cruising down the long lanes of selling humanity. Ten times he saw her stop before a basket, smell the eggs, ask the price and wander on. Then he lost sight of her. Perhaps she did eventually get a dozen eggs for one and four, but she had probably worn out three-pennyworth of shoe-leather in order to save one penny on eggs. That is the worst, he thought, of having an economical mind!

Romany told Sally Stordy of his experience, and she laughed heartily.

"That calls to mind summat that happened once," she said. "A woman came round and looked at my basket. 'I want a dozen eggs,' she said, 'that have been laid by black hens'. Well, I didn't know which had been laid by black or which had been laid by white, so I told her to pick her own if she knew the difference atween 'em. Well, she began sorting through 'em, and when she'd got her dozen she said, 'Them are a'reet'. As she paid me for 'em, I said to her, lookin' at the eggs, 'It seems to me that black hens lay all the biggest eggs'. 'Aye,' she said as she turned away. 'That's how ye tell 'em' ".

It was on November 20th, 1943, that the light which had shone so brightly was suddenly snuffed out. Romany had been digging in his garden for several hours and then went indoors to lie down and have a rest. Half an hour later his wife went through to see how he was and found that he had died in his sleep. As they said at the time, he had made his exit from life as he made his walks from one field to another – with hardly a sound.

The news of his death was broadcast on both the 6 o'clock and 9 o'clock News, and listeners all over the country were stunned, for they had lost a dear friend. The B.B.C. switchboard at Broadcasting House was jammed with calls, many from parents of distraught children worried that Raq might be left alone in the caravan. Hundreds of letters poured in from people in all walks of life, including the Armed Forces. It was a sad day for the many listeners for whom Romany had held out a candle over the Natural World.

Tangible tributes remained to his memory – a wall tablet in an animal clinic at Ilford, and a children's cot in a hospital in Birkenhead bearing the inscription:

From the B.B.C. Children's Hour
In Memory of Romany.
'He loved birds and green places and the wind on the heath,
and saw the brightness of the skirts of God'.

At Wilmslow, his caravan stood in a small public garden dedicated to Romany, with a display inside of poems written by children upon his death. One of these poems, written by a tearful young admirer, was broadcast on Children's Hour and expressed the feelings of many:

> They say he's dead, I say they lie,
> For such a man can never die.
> How dare they say a man is dead
> When his spirit lives on in his stead?
> Maybe his bones have turned to dust;
> He lives as live he surely must.
> He lives in every passing hour,
> In every tree and bud and flower;
> In every bird that sings a song,
> In every lane we walk along.
> His laughter echoes through the trees.
> His voice breathes softly in the breeze.
> He lives, and will immortal be:
> Our woodland friend – dear Romany.

Perhaps the greatest memorial of all lies in the memories of the many people who went ... Out With Romany.

And yet, I have a strong feeling that he, himself, left his own epitaph for, after his death, a piece of paper was found in his wallet. On it he had scribbled the following words:

> *Nobody ever grows old simply by living a number of years.*
> *Years wrinkle the skin, but to give up one's enthusiasm*
> *wrinkles the soul.*

Acknowledgements

This book owes much to the many old friends who have so willingly shared both memories and photographs with me. Those in the first group are too numerous to mention, but for assistance with illustrations I am particularly indebted to Lilian Anthony, Rhoda Bunn, Dennis Cross, Ernie Filby, Pat Green, Jan and John Howell, Pam and Philip Standley, Edna Watling and Elsie Bugden, and Philip Yaxley.

A special word of appreciation goes to John Kett, not only for his kind foreword, but also for the great pleasure which his poetry has given me over the years.

Bob Bagshaw,
Wymondham,
October 1995.